The Tunnels
of
Wallingford

Fact or Fiction?

This historic English town with at least a thousand years of history. What lies beneath?

Nick A. Shepherd

DEDICATION

To all the people of Wallingford, England. It used to be in Berkshire but now it's Oxfordshire –
no matter!

Especially to the friends that I grew up with in Wallingford, many of whom are still there, unlike my wife and I who "fled the nest." Yet the town and its memories remain in our hearts.

Finally, to my family: To my wife, my two Wallingford-born daughters and my son, the one original Canadian among us. Thanks to all of you for the love and inspiration.

Contents

ACKNOWLEDGEMENTS

I could not have completed this investigation without the help of many people.

Thanks to my friends who grew up with me in Wallingford – for the stories, adventures, and antics we shared.
Thanks to my grandparents, Leonard and Alice Shepherd, and my parents Arthur Shepherd and Edna (nee Watson); to all those who worked for the family grocery business, Leonard Shepherd Ltd., on High Street, as well as the hairdressing business; to my wife, Janet (nee Johnstone), who – like me – grew up in Wallingford; to her parents, Maurice and Marion and the rest of the Johnstone family, who owned Reynolds and Johnstone – known as R&J's – on St. Mary's Street; and to all the staff who worked there, especially Margaret Giles, one of the best sources of Wallingford information.

Special "shout outs" and thanks to Kenny Lester and Ros, Chris Johnstone and Frances Watkins, Marilyn Leadbetter (nee Johnstone) and Eric, Paul Crudgington and Jenny, David Ridge and Nina, and many others. Thanks also to my cousin, Christine (Bunty) Romine (nee Shepherd), for her personal memories and those of her sisters from when she lived at Flint House.

Finally, thanks to Wallingfordian's past and present for all the stories that you shared with me on social media; to Judy Dewey of Wallingford Museum both for the help and information and for having the passion to collect and assemble memories of Wallingford that may well have been forgotten; and to all those, who, because of their interest, have penned studies, stories and research about Wallingford and its history, especially the late John Kirby Hedges. The collective research from all of you, provides a little credibility to what I present here.

Wallingford? Where?

This book is about the "original" Wallingford in England, a town that developed around an important crossing point of the River Thames. There is evidence of Roman activity in the area which left traces of occupation, burials, roads, coins, and pottery. It appears that the name 'Wallingford' was first used in a Saxon charter of 821, where it appears as Wælingford. It also appears as Welingaford (891), and as Walingeford in the Domesday Book of 1086. Originally located in the royal county of Berkshire the town was transferred to Oxfordshire in the re-drawing of county boundaries in the 1970's. The major historic settlements, supported by evidence from archaeologists and geologists appears to be Saxon and medieval. But it is old - that is for sure.

Wallingford gained its Royal Charter in 1155; the Charter was granted by the great King Henry II in return for the support given to him by the town during the (then) recent civil war between his mother Empress Matilda and King Stephen. As an old, established English town, its' name was adopted in the new world; there are Wallingford's in several states in the USA - Connecticut (which is twinned by this Wallingford in England), Iowa, Illinois, Kentucky, Pennsylvania, Vermont, and Washington. There are also Wallingford's in New Zealand and Jamaica.

England has a wonderful history that is continually being updated and enlarged by the work of many volunteers and professionals. The town has a well established museum that houses many artifacts, and recently a scale model of Wallingford Castle was added. It also has an active "Town of Wallingford Historic and Archeological Society".

In its early days, Wallingford was a town of nobility with many portions of property owned by notable figures of royalty, the church and society. The original castle, built in 1067, was constructed on the direct instructions of William the Conqueror who had crossed the River Thames at Wallingford on his way to London to take the throne, and it stood and was active for several hundred years. The castle was expanded in the 13th century and later became a royal castle, strongly associated with many medieval kings. Parts of the actual castle still stand and are well worth a visit.

By nature, ancient towns evoke many stories about their past. So, it is with Wallingford. Whether because of its Castle or the towns' lengthy history, there have been many stories about tunnels and passageways that as yet lay unexplored beneath its streets. That is the subject of this book. Readers can make their own conclusions about whether tunnels may or may not be there - but this book at least captures some of the stories and ideas. Having been written down, maybe at some point in the future, explorers may unearth the truth!

Wallingford has a population of approximately 12,000 and is within easy reach of London.

Introduction

Are there tunnels underneath Wallingford? Undoubtably yes. However probably nowhere near the number and breadth that might be expected based on all the stories that have been passed down. But it does make for an interesting story.

I have been increasingly interested in this question as the years have passed and I arrived at the point where I wanted to try and find out a bit more. Although I was born in Didcot, soon after I was taken by my mother to live with her and my father, with his parents at Flint House. My grandfather purchased the property in 1916 from the Powys-Lybbe family (the same family that donated part of the land for the Bull Croft to the town of Wallingford). The Shepherds owned the property and lived there as the family home, until my grandfather died in 1955. My father then owned the property until the early 1960's. The Shepherd's had four children: Alec, the eldest, born in 1912; Hilda, born in 1915; my father Arthur, born in 1919; and Max, born in 1923. This is where my interest started, as there were stories about a tunnel from Flint House.

Over the years there have been conversations with friends about whether there are tunnels under Wallingford. Some felt strongly, some thought it was crazy, while others had seen "bricked up entrances" in the cellars of different houses in Wallingford. Some had even written about personal experiences and had been inside the actual tunnels. But it was just that – stories and hearsay.

In about 2020, during the lockdown due to the coronavirus (Covid-19) pandemic, I thought it would be a good idea to write a novel, centred in Wallingford at around 1100 or 1200, making use of the idea of tunnels as part of a story of two lovers, who used them to pass undetected to see each other. While this project is still in the formative stage, I did start to research how much was really known about the tunnels. I started out by posting a request for information on the "Bygone Wallingford" Facebook page. I was pleasantly surprised to receive over 100 replies, and this once again stirred the desire to find out more. While there were few real fact-based sightings, there were several stories that seemed to reinforce each other, as well as others that cast new light on potential areas to look into further. What to do next?

The challenge is that there are very few actual facts to support the existence of tunnels. However, there are a few that I believe are quite solid. There are lots of stories – as Judy Dewey commented "...if there are as many tunnels as there are stories, Wallingford would have collapsed many years ago!" I decided there were some avenues that I could follow up. First, the basic history of Wallingford settlements needs to be considered as a context for the existence of any tunnels, so I looked at that to try and obtain some background. It also started to become clear from the history that there had been settlements in Wallingford for well over a thousand years, during which time tunnels could have been created. Then I started to think about buildings that had existed for a long time; almost every building in Wallingford today dates from periods after the dates that tunnels might have been built, but what existed there before?

Although almost every building from the original settlements had been eliminated by fires set to level the town at least once, there were stories of some buildings, in particular churches, that were known to have stood on the site of former buildings from hundreds of years before. Maybe looking at church histories would give some clues, especially given the historic importance of the Church in earlier times and the potential for secret underground crypts and tunnels.

There has also always been a connection between stories about tunnels and Wallingford Castle. Sadly, little remains of the castle to verify these ideas, although there are accounts from over 100 years ago, of people who did experience at least one real tunnel. However, there are similar castles around the UK that were constructed around the same period as Wallingford Castle, where some level of remains still stand. Could comparisons with these buildings tell us anything about the possibility of tunnels under Wallingford?

This then was my journey and the foundations of what I can present in these few pages. It is for the reader to decide on the possibility or probability of either some tunnels, or an extensive network of them under Wallingford. Certainty can only come through more detailed investigation, including the willingness to open up some of the possible bricked-up tunnel entrances. Geophysical and other surveys may help, but in all probability the tunnels are too deep to clearly show up. For example, the recent archaeological dig at Wittenham Clumps demonstrated that little or no geophysical evidence does not always mean that there is nothing there. Maybe some selected drilling and video exploration in Wallingford might reveal something?

At least I hope that, here, I have been able to record the story telling and the few facts that exist for others to look in to. All one can hope for is an open mind and a willingness to see the possibilities.

What are the stories?

Story telling is an ancient art where one generation passes on information to the next; this used to be how history was built until we started to write things down. Today, many of us obtain answers from doing an internet search using Google, Chrome, Edge or any one of the browsers available to us. We can also use social media to ask others and tell our own story. More information is available to us today than ever before; what was written in books has been digitized, yet there remains a large volume of work that remains in the archives as the written word. Places like the Bodleian Library in Oxford have historical records going back hundreds of years, painstakingly catalogued and available to only a few with the time and willingness to explore.

So what? What does this mean for my search? Well, I am not a historian and I have neither the knowledge nor the experience to access a great deal of historical data that may be out there pertaining to Wallingford's history. So, I am sure that there remains a lot of material, which could further refine what I present. Secondly, history unfortunately goes to those who write it down; this means that some history is lost forever unless someone can excavate something that tells us something new. History also demonstrates that people come to different opinions based on their interpretation of the facts. Therefore, it is important for the reader to accept that I am unable to provide anything with certainty, especially where reputed specialists whose material I have reviewed, arrived at different conclusions. My apologies – but that is the nature of this type of work!

I also touched on story telling. While I believe this is an important avenue to pursue, it is also prone to problems. As human beings we tend to remember some things and forget others; as children, and even when we become adults, we tend to blur the lines between fictional stories and supporting facts. Many stories may be a combination of fiction woven around one or more key, central, valid facts. We also "out and out" make things up. We invent stories. The brain also sometimes tries to "connect the dots" by filling in the spaces in true stories with fiction to make the story line work (or make it better!). This is all to say that I started this journey using storytelling and tried to build from there, using the approach of "what supporting facts can I find" and "what is the probability that at least part of this could be true?" I also tried to ask myself what appears to be obviously in error.

There are stories

I have my own family stories, but we will come back to those later; the stories we start with fall into several categories. First let's start with one of the foundational stories of *The History of Wallingford* written by John Kirby Hedges in 1881[1]. We will come back to this, but it contains three documented stories of tunnels related to Wallingford Castle.

The History of Wallingford is extremely comprehensive. Volume 1 spends a great deal of time focusing on justifying Wallingford as Calleva which was a major Roman settlement near Silchester. When we look at the history, we see that Julius Caesar visited England for an "expeditionary visit" about 54 BC and then invaded in 43 AD, remaining in the country until about 410. In his references to this period, Hedges mentions tunnels in the Castle:

> About sixty years ago, some subterranean vaults and passages were excavated in the Castle grounds, which then belonged to the late Dr. Blackstone, Fellow of All Souls' College, Oxford, and one of the learned professors of that university, the masonry of which was pronounced by him and others to be undoubtedly Roman.

This suggests that the then owner of the Castle and grounds believed that beneath the buildings erected later there were tunnels relating back to the Roman period. Hedges tried to follow up on this later:

> In the year 1859, I traced a subterranean passage, probably the one referred to. It runs from the bottom of the keep on the south side, in the valley, and takes an easterly direction, rather inclining southwards, towards the river. It is of large size, and solid masonry, sufficiently large for a man to walk along, being about four feet high by two feet wide. The entire passage was effectually cleaned out and repaired up to its junction with the ditch, at or near the extremity of the Castle precincts. Beyond this point the passage could not be traced.

Later commentators suggested that there was an error in the writing related to the height of the tunnel. However, this tunnel would have headed towards the river approximately parallel to High Street. It may be, that this is the passage referred to, on an 1898 Ordnance Survey map of Wallingford that is clearly marked between the Castle and an area called Queens Arbour that fronted the west bank of the River Thames.

He also refers to another passage, also discovered by a previous owner of the Castle, that would appear to be related to the time frame when the main construction of Wallingford Castle had taken place although again, depending upon what was underneath the site, it is not impossible that this could also date back to earlier times.

About the year 1700, Thomas Renda, Esq., who then possessed the Castle, Manor and Honour of Wallingford, discovered on the north side of the keep, near the well spoken of by Camden as one of exceeding depth, and going in an eastward direction, a narrow passage between two walls, over which, apparently, there had been no covering. Mr. Skirmer remarks, " This passage has been supposed to pass under the Thames, and to come out on the opposite side of the river at a place called Dane Pits, in Crowmarsh Hill ; " but Dr. Blackstone, who explored the passage in 1820, notes—

" It appears to have no outlet from the Castle, but terminates in a staircase at each end, leading up to the buildings of the Castle ; but *under* it there is a narrower passage, leading from either staircase at the ends, . . . which appears like a dungeon—it is formed thus : —or prison. The walls of this are of Roman masonry.
J. B."

Here we have two possibilities: first a passage away from the Castle leading under the river to Crowmarsh and another, deeper down in the bowels of the castle leading to places unknown. Once again, the walls are identified as being "of Roman Masonry." Hedges was unwilling to affirm that the passages were "undoubtably Roman." Certainly, later archeological work has to some degree dispelled these stories - however as we will see later there is some similarity between these types of "lower passageways" which often led to dungeons and possible connections to tunnels. The new model of Wallingford Castle on display at the museum may help the "imaginative person" conjure up their own ideas!

Reference is made to these subterranean passages in this chapter, because they have been pronounced to be Roman, but we are not prepared, owing to the difficulty of making a careful examination of the masonry, to offer any corroborative testimony of the opinion of Dr. Blackstone, that they belong to the Roman period. That they were connected with the keep, and afforded a means of communication with points at a distance, for the purpose of supplying stores, or of escape, or to meet other military requirements, cannot be doubted; but it is by no means clear that the keep itself dates back beyond the time of the Conqueror, to whom, according to the prevailing authority, these artificial structures owe their origin or erection. If it be so, an argument may be raised that these passages, which are clearly connected with the keep at Wallingford, were not in existence anterior to the time of its construction. But on the other hand, it

Hedges makes the interesting point that "…they [the passages] were connected to the keep and afforded a means of communication with points at a distance, for the purpose of supplying stores, or of escape, or to meet other military requirements, cannot be doubted." This then provides a good foundation for a reason that tunnels under Wallingford may have existed, why they were there, and where they may have extended to. Remember, we are only dealing with stories here, although some of the above were written down by people who saw these passages with their own eyes. What we do appear to have is a *possible* connection to the Roman timeframe and a connection to the Castle.

In 1955, Wallingford celebrated its 800-year anniversary of the granting of the Royal Charter; my wife's uncle (James O. Johnstone, J.P.) was Mayor of Wallingford at the time, and his brother (my father-in-law, Maurice Johnstone[2]) was editor of the souvenir booklet. In the souvenir programme, he tells of a story (later re-printed in the Wallingford magazine and then in *"The Poor Man's Guide to Wallingford"* by Les Bullen):

One day about 55 years ago, beneath the cellar of 65 High Street, a room was discovered, in which was found a skeleton, armour, a sword, gauntlets and a mug. A wooden stool crumbled to dust upon touch. Further excavations in the garden led to the finding of a well shaft. It was thought possible that a tunnel led to the Castle, but expense made further excavations impossible.

History does not tell us the name of the unfortunate person who had been walled up and left to die, or perhaps just forgotten. In those barbaric days, centuries ago, it was easy to put an enemy into a dungeon and then forget. Unknown though he is, he will be remembered through the pages of this souvenir programme in the years to come.

Recent excavations in St. Martin's Street revealed further skeletons, but this time they had a Christian burial in what was possibly St. Martin's churchyard.

Space unfortunately does not permit further details, but one thing is certain - that beneath the pavements, streets and houses lies a storehouse of knowledge of Wallingford through the centuries.

Again, this was a souvenir programme for Wallingford's celebrations, and we do not see any corroborating facts. However, it is another story that has been repeated elsewhere. It also links to further stories and these fall into what I consider to be of four types – possible, questionable, unbelievable, and possible but out of context. Next, let's investigate what was found from the information collected from present-day Wallingfordian's.

These stories came from a review of four years of messages on the "Bygone Wallingford" Facebook group page. Initially, I posted a request for stories and received more than 100 replies; at that point I also conducted a search of all posts on the group site that mentioned either "passages" or "tunnels" and identified additional memories and stories from people. I then sorted these by general location and present the findings here in summary.

One of the first observations is that there are many stories centred around the eastern side of High Street from the Lamb crossroads to Wallingford Bridge, about cellars and tunnels underneath property on both the northern and southern sides of the street (the north being the Castle side). This would seem to make some sense, as this was probably the original settlement area close to the river; it is also where a large number of the properties are "listed buildings" and have preservation orders. Many of these stories came from different people and there appears to be some level of consistency among them. We are also fortunate in that there are some photographs of some of the bricked-up doorways in a few of the properties (thanks to Jon Webb).

Starting with the south side, which has the larger number of observations, we can see in the map below[3] (using Google maps as a base) that they cover the majority of properties. One of the challenges is that the numbers of the properties are in the process of being changed so that there are reports using both the old and new numbers. This seems to be a greater issue on the north (Castle) side.

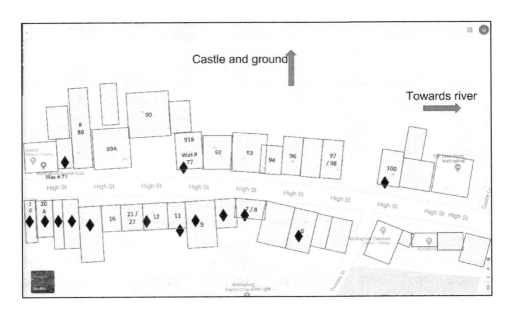

Each black diamond reflects one or more stories for that location.

No.	Current / old location	Comments
6	Calleva House	Arched, vaulted ceiling in cellars also featured.
7 - 11	Terraced Cottages	Mentioned 3 times one with specific reference to a tunnel bricked up in 1950s being unsafe.
16		Childhood memories of tunnel in cellar "...house next to Eagle House on the high street has a tunnel going through to the castle."
17 - 20	Terraced Cottages 2 with steps	Multiple mentions of family stories, also contractors who did work in cellars; pictures of bricked-up entrances. Data from "conservation listing" suggests that "...cellar of No.18 noted as having stone quadripartite vaulting of 2 bays, possibly incorporating re-used masonry from the priory church." In another reference "...my dad was born in the High St house in 1918 he said it had a vaulted cellar and a tunnel which may have been sealed up over the years."
23 - 24	Hair dressing salons	Reports by people having seen tunnel entrances "blocked up with bars" in the cellars.
77	Now numbered 91B	In the 1930s was Leonard Shepherd Ltd. Renovations in the 1950s revealed a cellar with old artifacts and a blocked-up door leading north.
88	Was Beisley Clockmakers	Story from contractor who did renovations in cellar of blocked-up doorway on north side.
100	Property next to Castle entrance	Report of closed-up tunnel entrance in cellar

The most numerous stories relate to 18 High Street, where there is also interesting linkage to the information provided for numbers 17, 18 and 19 in "British Listed Buildings". There are some further listings that extend up as far as the Lamb crossroads again shown on the base using Google maps[4]. There are several stories related to the upper end of High Street on both the south and north sides of the street.

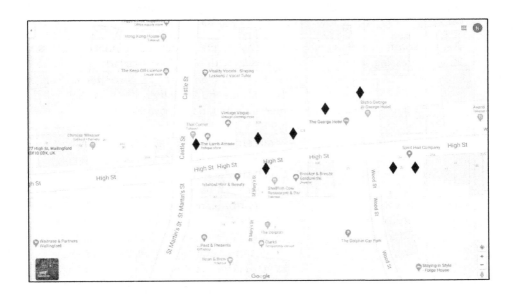

There have also been verbal suggestions that this is the area where the tunnels meet up and inter-connect – effectively east–west along High Street and then north to the castle (or other locations on the north side), as well as heading south into the town.

There is limited evidence and stories to support this, although, as will be discussed later, there was also the old St. Martin's Church on the southwest corner of the intersection, as well as All Hallows down Castle Street, with its graveyard on the East side (being the point where the supposed tunnel from the Lamb comes out). This area was the subject of a detailed excavation at the time of construction of the "new" Waitrose supermarket. The report makes interesting reading but alas, no tunnels!

There is no question that this is an old area of town, which includes historic properties like the George Hotel, so stories and speculation would be expected to have built around this older part of the town. The locations on the map are as follows:

23

No.	Current / old location	Comments
23 - 24	South side, Hair dressing salons	Reports by people having seen tunnel entrances "blocked up with bars" in the cellars.
1	St. Mary's Street	Added here as it abuts the house on the corner of High Street and St. Mary's Street. A past owner indicates that renovations revealed no tunnels.
	Lamb Hotel	Several references: one talked about having seen maps and stated, "One map showed a tunnel from the Lamb Hotel to the old churchyard just behind it ."
65	Now 82E, was Fergusons Wine and Spirit store	One story from late 1950s or early 60s from a person who knew owners and was taken to the cellar and saw the tunnel. Current owners confirm stories and suggest further that this links across the street with the tunnels on the south side as well as connecting to the Lamb.
	82B was National Westminster Bank	Stories about 65 High Street also allude to connections with tunnels that go beneath this property.
	George Hotel	Story about two entrances – one under the restaurant and one under the bar, both accessed through cellars.

There are also some photographs of bricked-up areas of cellars under houses in High Street; these examples come from no. 23, thanks to Jon Webb[5].

These, examples in themselves prove little, unfortunately: we need to see what is behind! There appears to be such a contradiction of different materials that there have been changes over an extended period of time. However, although we do not have other pictures, we do know that many locations that we have stories from report that there are either "bricked up doorways" or "entrances that have bars on" or others that have "been firmly closed off." The challenge is how to explore further – especially given that most of the properties on the south side of High Street have been designated as Grade II listed buildings.

There are also stories about tunnels from the western end of High Street – specifically Stone Hall, where there is one reference, and Flint House which will be dealt with separately. The next group of stories are limited and there are few corroborations; however, it is possible that if a network did extend under the town, then these locations may have reasons to be included.

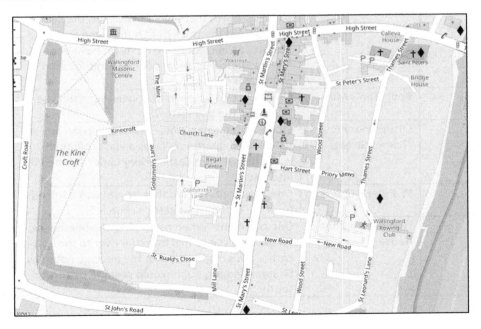

There are eight locations shown in the last map[6], of which four are around the Market Place and four are further out, although still within the original boundaries of the town. While the stories are scant, they are included as being worthy of consideration and speculation!

No.	Current / old location	Comments
1	St. Mary's Street	Added here as it abuts the house on the corner of High Street and St. Mary's Street. A past owner indicates that renovations revealed no tunnels.
18A	Market Place. KP Stationers, originally "The Feathers" pub	Story from contractor doing the renovations for KP who discovered a cellar. "The cellar runs long ways from the car park end and the door was in the far wall towards the Market Place."
6	St. Martins Street. Was Goodwin's and previously the "Eight Bells" pub	Story about personal memory: "...but I do remember being in the cellar under what was Goodwin's [the shop that is to the left of what was the post office] and there were bricked up passages down there too." (However, the Eight Bells was on the corner of Church Lane and St. Martin's Street. Given that it might have been St. Mary's Church House at one time this location seems more valid.)
	Boughton's Mill	One story of a tunnel having been seen (maybe related to the mill water?)
	Castle Priory / Thames Street	Story related to a tunnel – may have been access to servants' quarters? "I was always told there was a tunnel from Castle Priory under Thames St. into town."
	St. Peter's Church	One comment "I heard that [there] was a tunnel from the castle to St. Peter's church."
	Wallingford Boat House	One comment "When renovating the boathouse, I walked up the tunnel from the river to the castle." This might link with the passage noted by Sir John Hedges, but it would seem to be too far south.

Finally, there are the "out-of-towner" stories. These may seem impossible at first but could have a role to play, once again these are shown superimposed on the Google Map[7] below:

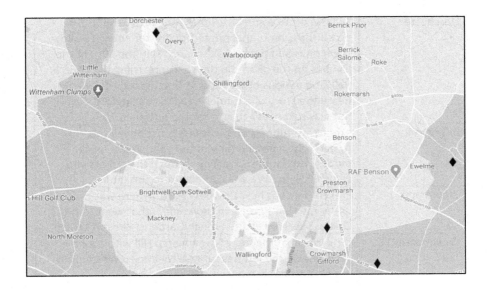

There are five stories, some of which contain more information than others, listed in the next table. However, it may be worth considering two things about these locations, before deciding whether they are "real."

Firstly, the use of words and expressions changes. In this case stories about tunnels might refer to something like the "Underground Railroad," for example, which was not a railway per se; in this case, "tunnels" might have referred to pathways that exited – maybe the Castle at some point, maybe a door or sallyport – and opened onto a "well-worn path" to these locations which had some connection with the Castle.

Secondly, these stories might have been partly made up of facts about some portion of tunnels, especially up to the exit point, such as a short tunnel under the bailey ending outside the defences. (It is interesting that the bottom of the moats appeared to be made of solid materials which would have made them somewhat waterproof.)

Current / old location	Comments
Dorchester	Two separate comments (one from each "end"): "[I] heard that one tunnel ran to Dorchester abbey to allow the monks and priests to escape..."; "In the 50s I lit the candles on the altar, did the collection, rang the church bell, and various other tasks at Dorchester Abbey – I'd heard the story of a tunnel going to Wallingford Castle, but was told never to go near the entrance."
Brightwell	"There are tunnels in Brightwell cum Sotwell too. Apparently, a certain time of the year, you can see monks with lanterns walking through the streets and vanish!" Hmm. We will come back to this later.
Crowmarsh 1	French Gardens new Howbery Park. "There was one under my Nan's house in Crowmarsh that went to the Castle. She lived at The French Gardens, Benson Lane."
Crowmarsh Hill	"The house at the top of Crowmarsh Hill with a long driveway on the left has tunnels that go to Wallingford but also probably blocked off."
Ewelme	"I was always told there was one from the castle to Ewelme church." (There are several churches in Ewelme clustered close together.)

The potential for connections to outlying points would depend heavily on the period when these routes might have been created and used. This will be explored in the later chapter on the historical and archaeological linkages.

Flint House: Where my interest began

Finally, let's look at the stories about Flint House. I lived here until I was about 5 years old and visited until I was about 16. I remember little about when I was a child living there but I do remember the latter years, especially after my grandfather died in 1954 and I visited the property on a regular basis as my father had converted it to a warehouse for his grocery wholesale business (terrible waste!). My father lost possession in about

1963 or 64 and died in 1966.

There are two sets of stories and I start with my own recollections. When I first lived there with my parents, our living room was on the left as you came in the front door and you then entered a passage[8] (the main living room was on the right, and the kitchen was straight ahead).

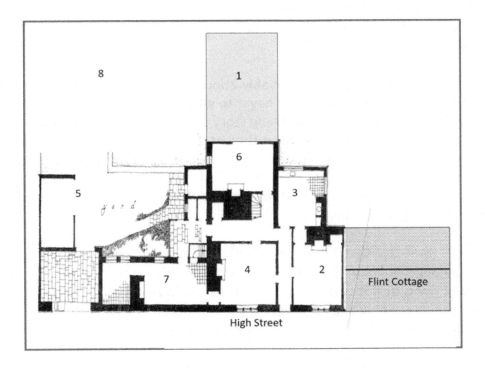

The property itself extended across what is today the entrance to the library and car park and connected to the large two-storey house next door. Leading off my parent's flat was a door by the fireplace that led into a "scullery" that was almost an outbuilding and contained the old washing tubs and a mangle, and much of what today would be kept in a utility room. Leading from this scullery was a door opening to a stairway that led to the cellars below, which can be seen on the schematic.

The numbers depict the following: (1) was a modern extension my father added for the business as a storeroom laid on what was the grass lawns; (2) was the main living room; (3) the kitchen; (4) my parents' living room (for a few years and I think it was also used as a dining room); (5) was the yard which was accessed from double doors leading on to High Street across a cobbled walkway (there was a massive Yew tree in the centre of the yard); (6) was a private living room with a beautiful bay window that my father demolished when the store was added; (7) was the scullery with the stairs adjacent to the chimney; and (8) was the extensive walled garden that backed on to the Bull Croft.

When I was older – probably about 12 – I did venture down the cellar stairs, but I had been told never to go down there, being warned of ghosts. I was also told the following story about a door and tunnel by my mother, who apparently had seen the entranceway. "The is a doorway in the cellar that opens into a tunnel that runs into Wallingford and connects to the Castle and to the old mint that used to be on Goldsmith's Lane." At the time, the cellars were used for storage of boxes and old furniture, as well as being a coal cellar.

I was told that, when my grandfather had purchased the property, the passage had been closed off (I do not remember whether there was a sealed door, or if it was bricked up). They had opened it up and found a passageway behind and a few feet inside a skeleton of what was said to be a younger man. They entered the tunnel and went quite some distance until they once again found the tunnel closed off. At this point there was another skeleton, which was of a young woman. The story was that the two had been lovers and had been using the tunnel to secretly meet. They had been found out and each end had been closed up while they were inside. Some story! However, having the tunnel unblocked would seem to support a later story that I heard from my cousin, Bunty.

My uncle, Alec Shepherd, who had grown up in Flint House, had married in 1933 and had three daughters, Diane, Jill, and Christine (who was called Bunty). Alex joined the glider regiment and in 1943 was killed in the Sicily landings. His wife and daughters had moved in with his parents at Flint House. My grandmother had been continually pestered by these young granddaughters to show them the "passages in the cellar" and so Bunty, several years later wrote the following account:

"Being the grand-daughter of Alice and Leonard Shepherd I spent many days and nights at Flint House; my father was the oldest of their four children and our family lived at Flint House with my grand-parents before the war. One day in particular, stands out in my mind. If I were to hazard a guess, I would place the time around the winter of 1944-45, as my family left Wallingford in 1945 before the war ended. My sister Diane would have been about eleven years old, Jill ten and myself around eight.

On this particular day, we were all inside, which supports the probability that it was wintertime; we were up on the second floor of the house having a great time, knocking on the panelling searching for secret rooms or priest holes. We came to a door in the panelling that opened onto a stairway to the upper floor (the "attic"). As we stood there arguing as to which one of us would be the first one to go up the stairs, Grandma Shepherd came along. She became upset when she saw that we were planning to go up the stairs and forbid us to EVER go up there. We begged and pleaded with her to just let us have a little peak, asking her to go with us but nothing we said would move her.

Finally, she said "we will have to settle this once and for all." She gave strict instructions to "stay where we were and not move" then left to return a short time later with a set of keys with which she promptly locked the door. Not ones to give up we persisted in asking her why we could not go to the top floor; possibly as a means of distraction she then said "I want you to promise me that you will NEVER go up those stairs? Promise me that if you ever find the door open you will come and tell me, then I will show you something." Of course, we promised.

Grandma then took us downstairs to the cellars at Flint House; the door led from the back kitchen to a set of stairs down into the cellar; we went down the stairs into what appeared to be an ordinary cellar but then we reached the entrance of what seemed to be older cellars. At this point Grandma realized she had forgotten to bring her torch, so she left the three of us wandering around the cellars, wondering what she was going to show us. When she returned with the torch and before we went any further, she told us that she wanted a promise from each of us that we would never tell anyone what she was about to show us. We all promised that we would not tell but it appeared that was not good enough for Grandma, so she asked each of us individually to make the promise. All went well until it got to me; I made my promise and added "except for Pam." Pam was Pamela Phillips my best friend to whom I told everything. I was told I must not tell Pam either; for the longest time I refused to make the promise, so Di and Jill asked Grandma to take them and leave me behind, but Grandma said, "we all go, or nobody goes." So finally, after being pressured by my sisters, I promised not to tell Pam.

We went on into the older part of the cellars; these appeared to have been the foundations of the monastery over which Flint House was built. These cellars seemed darker and danker; against one wall there were many boxes stacked haphazardly on top of one another. Di, Jill, and I helped Grandma clear these boxes away which took quite a time. Behind the boxes was an old door which Grandma opened with one of her keys. We could see a passage behind the door; Grandma took Jill and I in first; she told Di that if too much time went by and we didn't come out of the tunnel, she was NOT to come into the tunnel but to go and get help as the tunnel was falling down in places.

As she took Jill and I into the tunnel it appeared that the floor, walls, and ceiling were all made out of dirt; I think there was some kind of bracing, but I can't be sure. We went in for quite a way and in places we could see little slides and piles of dirt where it had fallen. Too soon (for us) Grandma took us back out again. Now it was Di's turn and Grandma said she would take Di in a bit further so they would be gone a little longer. She said that if we started to get worried then we should go for help. Finally, as we waited, we could see the light from their torch and hear their voices as they made their way back to us and closer to the entrance.

Di told us that Grandma had taken her down the tunnel to a place where there was a fork; I remember that she had said that one fork led to the castle, but I cannot remember where the other tunnel went. For some reason I seem to remember that it may have been Calleva House, but it also may have been the Town Hall or the old mint.

It was an experience that I have never forgotten. There are cellars under Flint House, and there was definitely a tunnel leading from the cellars that ran under the town to Wallingford Castle and forks off in another direction at some point. I know because I was in it.

My promise not to tell Pam lasted about two months; for an eight-year-old a secret passage was just too delicious a secret to keep from my best friend! Pam lives in Australia, and I don't know if she remembers me telling her about it as she was younger than me but maybe I will ask her when I write to her next time.

Some may discount this as the "creative memory of a child," but it seems to have some level of a ring of truth to it. It is possible that soon after this occurred the tunnel entrance was closed up. However, looking at the front of Flint House, you can still see the entrance to the cellars where coal and other items were stored.

This picture[9] shows both Flint House and Flint cottage (on the right) in 1937 when they were decorated by my grandparents for the coronation of King George VI and Queen Elizabeth. Today, the single-story extension to the building shown on the left no longer exists, having been demolished in the early 1960s. However, beneath the left ground floor window, can be seen the grille that opened up to the cellars.

Soon after my grandfather died and my father took over the property, several renovations were undertaken to convert the whole interior to a wholesale storage building. A large amount of rubble was created that was all disposed of down the cellar; thus, from the late 1950s any further access to the area was impossible.

As an aside to the tunnels story, my father had grown up in Flint House and slept in the upstairs back bedroom, shown as 6 in the diagram of the upstairs layout (based on the same information as endnote "8" - the door and stairs to the attic that my cousin mentioned is also shown as 7).

High Street

Apparently, my father suffered many dreams and nightmares as a child sleeping in this room; it may well be that he had the rubble thrown into the basement to ensure that no one could access the tunnels as a way to deal with some lingering fears he may have had. We will never know. The combination of rumours about tunnels at both Stone Hall and Flint House is interesting, especially given their location and the history of the site.

So, there we have the collection of stories, rumours, dreams, and other recollections, many of which have contributed to the continuing belief that there are tunnels under the town of Wallingford. While there are stories, we have little proof. However, we do have several stories from contractors involved in renovations and these might carry additional weight.

Sadly, there is little left of the Castle to play a role in proving that tunnels existed; additionally, Wallingford has stood on this site for well over a thousand years, so the potential for tunnels could involve many cycles of building, destruction, renovation, and rebuilding, layer upon layer. While there have been several archeological digs in Wallingford, both as projects and initiated by new developments, few have revealed anything about tunnels – but also few have probably gone deep enough to satisfy the possibility of incredibly old tunnels.

There are many Grade I and Grade II listed buildings in the centre of Wallingford reflecting the history of Wallingford. As mentioned earlier, many of these are the same buildings where people have stories about hidden passages. The following map shows how the "centre" of the town appears to have remained the same. The darker shadings reflect those properties that are listed.

It might be interesting for the reader to refer back to this page at the end of the book to see a correlation between listed buildings and possible tunnels. While any connection is pure speculation, it is an indicator that the areas in town considered "historically important" have been so for many years. These materials are publicly available and provide a good context for understanding both the history of Wallingford as well as plans for the future. This chart[10] shows the large number of buildings designated as historically important, which are shown as darker images.

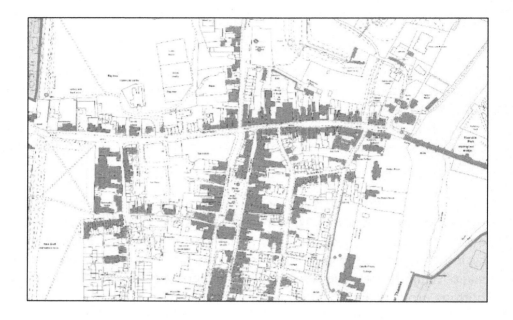

Thus, we are left looking for other sources of information to either support speculation or prove that it is impossible for these tunnels to exist. This we will address next, but before we do a few words on the evolving nature of understanding what is "beneath Wallingford" from a more evidence and factual base.

Geology and Archeology

Wallingford has been identified as an early settlement in Britain and has held importance for a long time because of both its location on the route between London and the west country, but also because of its ford across the River Thames. The result is that there are hundreds of years of history, most of which has limited visible evidence. Sure, the ruins of Wallingford Castle clearly demonstrate the existence of a castle from decades ago, but little is left standing. The earthworks around the Kine Croft and Bull Croft also clearly demonstrate early protective works and fortifications around the town. While few old buildings are left standing, there remain many that can trace histories back several hundred years; this is especially true of the three main remaining churches that are also on sites that date back hundred's if not a thousand years. It is also true of Flint House, now the site of Wallingford Museum. We know that the town was granted its' Charter in 1155 noting it as a place of special value and importance to the King. We also have lots of stories handed down from generation to generation. History is often based on storytelling and Wallingford has lots of stories.

However when it comes to facts to support the history, we must rely on specialist work carried out by the many researchers including geologists, archeologists and others who dedicate themselves to looking "below the surface" in search of buried parts of buildings and other items that might either substantiate theories about the towns history or serve as pieces of a puzzle that can start to connect the dots and increase or substantiate the probability of certain stories, theories and ideas of the past. This was clearly the case when, over a hundred years ago there were beliefs that Wallingford was the site of Calleva Atrebatum, a significant Roman settlement; over the ensuring period the work the professionals is believed to have proven that this theory was incorrect and that, while Wallingford may have had some level of Roman presence, Calleva was in fact near Silchester.

Likewise, the work of people such as Neil Christie, David Roffe, and especially Katharine Keats-Rohan in researching the history of Wallingford Castle have added considerably to the understanding of the past and the revelation of facts that support a clearer idea of what really happened. As interest in Wallingford's history has grown, technology has become more capable and as more people have volunteered to help in "digs and excavations" an increased level of facts are becoming available. The Town of Wallingford Historical and Archeological Society (TWHAS) founded in 1973 has done much to move this agenda forward; an example is following up on the suggestion of Professor Neil Christie of Leicester University, who led The Wallingford Burh to Borough Project from 2008-2011, to dig a series of 100 "test pits" in various locations around Wallingford, including their gardens. This work is now finished and, in the writing, and publication stage, but there is no evidence of test pits revealing voids that might have been tunnels! All of this work helps provide factual evidence but to date none has confirmed tunnels under the town or suggested areas of interest that might be close to or once have been hidden passageways. The last twenty years have also clearly revealed that Wallingford's major heritage is Saxon and medieval.

Judy Dewey, a champion of Wallingford's history and a member of the TWHAS, is curator of Wallingford Museum and has been the driving force in many of the initiatives, projects and programs aimed at enhancing knowledge of the town. In relation to the possibility of tunnels, Judy mentioned that *"In the 1970s/80s Alan Brodrick (a TWHAS member with architectural background) did quite a thorough cellar survey in the centre of the town, but sadly he passed away before he wrote it up. We have his notes in the archives and I now feel that we should certainly revisit them. I personally think it is the cellars of our older buildings that are the basis of most of the 'stories'; many of them seem to be childhood memories, where dark cellar storage areas can rapidly turn into blocked up tunnels."* Additionally, Judy points out the geology of Wallingford might suggest that tunnels are improbable, as much of the ground is composed of gravel which would have made tunneling a challenge.

The only way that proof can be obtained is to get some more factual evidence of the tunnels. As the work of the experts moves forward maybe this might be revealed in the future - but so far nothing of substance. Hopefully one day some of the doorways may be opened up and excavations made in areas of interest? BUT - we do have stories and theories! Let's look at those.

Context for Tunnels

In seeking corroboration of the stories about tunnels in Wallingford, several sources can be explored. We have some stories that suggest the tunnels may date back to Roman times, while it is not impossible that they could have been built later; or maybe some were built in the time of Roman occupation but expanded later. Maybe there were no tunnels until Wallingford Castle underwent its main development and construction after 1066 and they were created as part of this? We will never know definitively but in this chapter, we can explore "possibility."

I am not either an historian or an archeologist and my knowledge is extremely limited; as for any storyteller, there are those who will look at my words and suggest I have used the facts to support a certain set of beliefs. I hope not; rather, I hope to be able to present enough information for it at least to be interesting. There are many smarter, more learned, and more experienced people who have researched many of these topics. I recommend the reader to explore these materials as widely as they desire; I am not going to re-write them or dispute them in any way. I have just selected pieces as "food for thought."

The Context of Wallingford History
When starting this story, I thought that, because I grew up in Wallingford, I knew about the town. I was quickly proven wrong. Wallingford is a

treasure trove of fascinating history. Credit must go the Judy Dewey and the TWHAS (Town of Wallingford Historical and Archaeological Society) for the work that they do to preserve the past and inform for the future. Thanks, must also go to everyone who has contributed in some way to collecting and retaining information about the history of Wallingford. If not for their valiant efforts, our history would be forgotten; alas there are already many gaps.

Also, in doing my limited research, I realize that different people, reviewing similar facts may have come to different conclusions. Nowhere is this more evident than in the detailed research and writings of John Kirby Hedges in his two volumes of *The History of Wallingford*, much of the first volume being dedicated to substantiating his belief that Wallingford was a major centre of Roman settlement. In spite of his research and obvious belief, further work by others has failed to provide adequate facts to substantiate his arguments, either through historical research or different interpretations of the same source materials, nor from evidence from unearthed archeology. Yes, Wallingford may have been a Roman settlement although there is little evidence, but not to the extent that Hedges originally believed. Looking at the overall context, there is a LONG history.

Age[11]	Dates	Comments
Bronze Age	2100–750 BC	Although there are records of tunnels and earthworks this seems a low probability period for Wallingford.
Iron Age	750 BC–AD 43	
Roman	43–410	Lower probability - Romans did build tunnels but little Wallingford evidence.
Sub-Roman	410 – c. 450	
Saxon	c. 450–793	Low probability as there appear few references to tunnels built in this era. Possible though.
Viking	793–1066	
Norman / Medieval	1066–1485	Higher probability as many castles were being built with tunnels and there remained social conflict.

Age[11]	Dates	Comments
Tudor	1485–1603	Medium to high probability related to religious persecution.
Stuart	1603–1714	Medium to low probability; although tunnels would have been built, it is probably for commercial purposes with the beginning of water supplies, sewers, transport, and other purposes. There is also a higher likelihood of records.
Georgian	1714–1837	
Victorian	1837–1902	
Modern	1902–	

One of the most important considerations is asking why tunnels might have been constructed. From this perspective things in society have changed little. There has to be a good reason to build a tunnel, which would have required financial resources to pay people and to acquire materials. Even if the tunnels were built by people "already being paid" – such as soldiers or other workers, these would still have been resources that could have been put to alternative use.

Why then would tunnels be built? In simple terms to allow access – for people to come and go unseen (or be protected). They can also be built for services – water, sewage etc. Additionally, more in modern times, to avoid congestion. Based on this thinking we can then look at the various time periods and ask, "would these people have built tunnels and if so, for what purpose?" We will look at the Roman era as a starting point.

Thoughts from Roman Times
Wallingford was a settlement long before Roman times, as the Wallingford Museum website[12] explains:

"It was the river that first attracted settlers to the area and in the Bronze and Iron Ages the rich soils encouraged farming communities. The Romans in turn left traces of occupation - burials, roads, coins, and pottery, but it was left to the Anglo-Saxons to build the first town.

Note that the museum says, "left traces" only; the Romans were well known for taking the experiences that had developed "back home" and deploying them across their Empire. However there remains scant geological or archeological evidence that Wallingford was a significant Roman location. While some finds of pottery and coins have been found, the consensus appears to be that the location would not have been of a size that merited making a significant effort to create tunnels. However, there are a few observations:

1. The layout of the town is similar to other Roman settlements based on a grid with a central crossroads and meeting area, similar to Silchester (Calleva), and St. Albans.

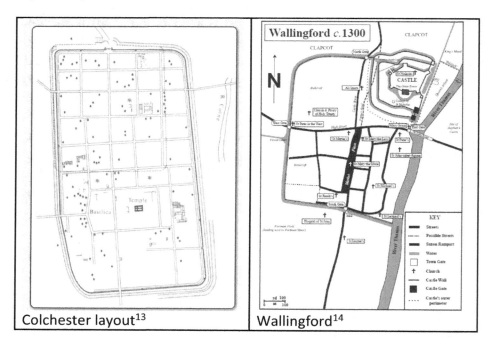

Colchester layout[13]   Wallingford[14]

2. Goldsmith's Lane suggests that this location may have been the area of the original mint. It has been suggested that once the Castle was built the "mint" was moved within its walls for protection (so prior to that it must have been outside the walls, certainly in Saxon times if not before).

3. Much of the evidence presented by Kirby Hedges suggests that Wallingford was a significant settlement for the Romans. The reader is referred to the arguments in Volume 1 (see endnote 1). However extensive archeological work both in Wallingford and Silchester would seem to invalidate this argument.
4. Wallingford was a major crossing point of the Thames and is located (as Hedges suggests) at the crossing points for east–west and north–south travel. (Although the crossing point may not have been where the bridge is today).
5. Remains of Roman Villas have been found in the Cholsey area[15] and in 2020 as part of a dig at Wittenham Clumps[16]
6. Wittenham Clumps has been identified as one of the topographical high points at which the Romans positioned signalling fires as an "early warning system" of impending invasions.
7. The Wittenham Clumps dig in 2020 also seems to indicate there was a "significant" Roman settlement in the area – could this have been part of a larger settlement area spreading through Brightwell to Wallingford?
8. IF the Romans had any significant settlement, it is likely that what is now the Castle grounds may have been used by them; also, in spite of his lack of factual support for Roman building materials at Wallingford Castle, Kirby Hedges writes that previous owners had dated some of the stonework as Roman.
9. It has been stated[17] that St. Mary's Church might have been originally built on the site of an ancient Roman basilica (although again this appears to have been invalidated by recent renovations).

In addition to speculating on what was happening around Wallingford, we can do some comparisons with similar periods of time elsewhere in England. It is believed that the Romans did build castles. As an example, in about 290 AD castles were built in an area known as the Saxon Shore forts that included Pevensey, Dover and Portchester. These locations were to defend the shores of England and became the sites for later forts in the Norman era that are known to have tunnels. Could these tunnels have been built by the Romans?

Lincoln[18] was also the site of an old Roman fortress built during the occupation, somewhere between 43 and 400 AD (probably later in the period, maybe around 300 AD). Many Roman towns of any size had a Forum which contained a Basilica; a basilica was an ancient Roman public building, where courts were held, as well as serving other official and public functions. One was discovered at Lincoln, so is it possible that there was a similar forum and basilica in Wallingford in Roman times, if the original foundation of St. Mary Le More was built on one? Certainly, the Market Place, as it is today – and might have been at that time – appears to be the central open, gathering area. There are stories of tunnels in Lincoln, so could these in any way date back to the Roman period?

The Silchester site, alleged to be the major Roman settlement of Calleva, which has been extensively explored and appears to never have been built over (i.e., a "green field" site), might have been an ideal location to find tunnels had they been built by the Romans as part of their towns in that period. Alas, it appears that no trace has been found.

Dover Castle, identified as one of the Roman sites from about 300 AD, has an extensive history of passages built underneath. This site may date much earlier and have been fortified with earthworks in the Iron Age before the Romans invaded in AD 43. (This is suggested on the basis of the unusual pattern of the earthworks which does not seem to be a perfect fit for the medieval castle.) Excavations[19] have provided evidence of Iron Age occupation within the locality of Dover Castle, but it is not certain whether this is associated with the hillfort. However, once again, although the castle has tunnels there is no indication that these date to Roman times or before.

Pevensey Castle has stories of tunnels but, once again, although the site was a fort in Roman times, there is no indication that any of the tunnel's date from that period. A similar story exists for Portchester Castle[20] that started as a Roman fort in the third century. Once gain, although it was expanded by the Saxons and became the base of one of the strings of Norman castles that we will discuss later, there is no indication that any tunnels existed from that period.

The only other speculative thought on the Roman period relating to Wallingford is that if (and it is a BIG if) there was a significant Roman settlement at Wallingford and IF there was indeed a basilica under where St. Mary Le More church stands, then it might be possible that one of the suspected tunnels in the area of Church Lane and St. Martin's Street could be a connection between the basilica and another building that pre-dated what later possibly became St. Mary's Church house.

One could further speculate that this same tunnel was in some way connected to both the tunnel found during the KP renovations, in the Market Place and even a location on the other side under what is now the Corn Exchange. Could these all have been a Roman network linking a number of key buildings? To add to this speculation, if one looks at the shape of the roadways around St. Mary Le More Church towards both Church Lane and the pathway at the side of KP leading to the car park behind Waitrose (Feathers Yard), they appear to slope away from the Market Place. Roman street building tended to reflect this with the centre continuing to be built higher so as to allow the water to drain away to the sides.

What can probably be concluded is that there is truly little evidence to suggest that any tunnels under Wallingford, even if they exist, were created at the time of the Roman occupation.

What happened after the Romans left?

Well, from the story of tunnels, probably little happened after the Romans left. As the Historic UK timeline[21] of the Roman occupation indicates, "AD 410 – With increased incursions from the Saxons, Scots, Picts and Angles, Britain turns to the Roman emperor Honorius for help. He writes back telling them to 'look to their own defenses' and refuses to send any help. This letter marked the end of Roman Britain. In the vacuum of power left *by the Romans, various individuals established themselves as territorial rulers and 'tribes' once again became the way people were grouped. Different areas faced incursions from both offshore and from neighbouring tribes."*

However, there was one ongoing trend that might be of interest to our story on tunnels and this was Christianity. Although there is not a great deal of history on the development of Christianity, some more recent studies[22] have demonstrated the many Roman Emperors had converted to Christianity and this impacted their occupation of England. *"When the Romans withdrew from Britain in the early fifth century, they not only left behind a vast Roman culture, but also a religion, Christianity, which was inherently Roman. ...new research has proven that Christianity was not solely an urban, upper-class phenomenon. Instead, it had widespread appeal throughout Britain and elicited a deep commitment from its adherents, which allowed Christianity to persist even through the pagan attacks of the fifth century AD and beyond."*

Initially, when the Romans arrived, they believed in the classical gods of the Graeco-Roman world, such as Jupiter, Juno, and Minerva, and even the divine majesty of the emperor. These were honoured and worshipped at temples in the cities of Britain, and at the forts of the army stationed in the province. However, this changed over time as the Romans were tolerant of other religions and then fully embraced Christianity after Constantine was converted in 312 AD. Even before the Romans left, the Christian Church was still undergoing persecution and there were efforts to eliminate Christianity. However even by this stage churches had been built in England both in cities and in rural areas. This included Silchester, Canterbury, Caerwent and possibly others. Three English Bishops attended meetings in Rome in 314 AD as official representatives.

The "churches" that developed took various forms, from the conversion of previous Celtic worshipping locations to Christian churches; to places of workshop in or adjacent to Roman villas as well as the creation of "new buildings." It appears that the form of building did not necessarily follow any historic architectural "norm" at this stage, thus the identification of such buildings can be difficult. But they were there.

With the arrival of the Saxons there were efforts to eliminate Christianity, until it started to re-emerge with St. Augustin in 600 AD, after which he created the Archdiocese of Canterbury and the religion spread once again. Once more the construction of churches started as the religion spread around the country. Stories of old tunnels appear to be often linked with ancient churches.

Secrets of the Early Churches

Knowing that the late Roman and early Saxon periods were a time of developing Christianity, we might look further into the possibility of tunnels and passageways being connected to the early development of churches. While no specific discoveries of tunnels in Wallingford have been connected to churches, there is local history that demonstrates that there were established churches dating to this time. Research might show us whether there are similar locations in England where there are linkages.

The first such example is from Hertfordshire. The "Hitchin tunnels" mentions connections between the Priory (and other locations at a later date) and St. Mary's Church. *"This is the largest parish church in Hertfordshire[23]. Most of the church dates from the 15th century, with its tower dating from around 1190. During the laying of a new floor in the church in 1911, foundations of a more ancient church building were found. In form, they appear to be a Basilican church of a 7th-century type, with a later enlarged chancel and transepts, perhaps added in the 10th century. This makes the church older than the story (not recorded before the 15th century) that the church was founded by Offa, king of Mercia 757-796."*

The second example is from Lincoln[24]: *"There are few attested late Roman Christian churches in Britain, and Lincoln has a claim to being the site of one. The archaeological evidence is not currently conclusive, but a series of churches excavated within the courtyard of the Roman forum may have originated in the 4th Century. The excavation of the Roman forum between 1972 and 1978 was enabled through the demolition of the church of St Paul in the Bail. That last church on the site was of Victorian date, itself a replacement for earlier Georgian and Medieval churches. The excavations revealed traces of even earlier churches in the sequence, and of possible physical connections to the Roman forum structure. The second church in the sequence was of a simple apsidal form of 7th Century date, and its outline is marked out on the surface of the modern St Paul in the Bail."* (There is a current photograph, showing the location of the church as well as a drawing of what it might have looked like on the website.)

There are additional examples of churches from this period and explanations on the Great English Churches website[25]. Firstly *"at Brixworth in Northants; the wooden church was rebuilt in stone between AD750–850. There was an apse, a nave, a tower and even porticus's – side chapels – along both sides of the nave. This was clearly a Romanesque design."* They also mention Deerhurst in Gloucestershire. This had an apse, traces of which can still be seen. These churches were in the precincts of the ancient Kingdom of Mercia, not its great northern rival Northumbria. Only monks could afford to procure the materials and the skilled workforce to build in stone. They could do so only through patronage because the monks of the day were extremely poor. Only centuries later would the monastic orders forsake their vow of poverty.

So, the Anglo-Saxon churches we see today would all have been built under the patronage of local kings or lords. These connections to the Kingdom of Mercia are interesting as the Thames at Wallingford was the border between the Kingdoms of Wessex and Mercia – so the possibility of churches exists. Also, the comment *"...built under the patronage of local kings or lords"* would support the idea that an area like Wallingford, which by this time in history was a leading settlement with several "monied" landowners, had a rich potential for the development of church related buildings.

This brings us back to a possible Wallingford connection. The town had many churches that had developed over the years; based on available records, the locations may date back to churches built in the pre-Norman era over ruins from the late Roman or Saxon era. There are four churches that might have possible history before the Norman times and before the Castle was built:

St. Mary-the-More / St. Mary Le More (Mother of all Churches)	Market Place	Built soon after the Norman Conquest (c. 1066), the oldest Christian Church in town. 1653: Tower rebuilt with materials from the castle. Advowson (patronage) belonged to St. Albans Abbey including 1075 the right to appoint Rectors. 1160: The Church passed to the Priory of Holy Trinity, daughter House of St. Albans Abbey. *Maybe built on original site of Roman Basilica*
St. Leonard's or aka Holy Trinity the Lesser	St. Leonard's Street	Old Anglo-Saxon church destroyed by the Danes in 1006 originally known as Holy Trinity the Lesser; *maybe dates back to the 6th century (St. Mary website)* Rebuilt soon after 1066 apparently by Robert D'Oyley (appears it might pre-date the burgh wall?). 1646: served as barracks for troops in the Civil War. Damaged by fire 1646, repaired and restored c. 1700, enlarged 1850. United with St. Mary-le-More
St. Martins	Centre High / Castle	Southwest of St. Mary-le-More; 1298: John Fisher, Rector; 1396: Hugh Roches last Rector; church dilapidated by 1412. *Excavations (new Waitrose site) showed Saxon burials c. 410 – 1066*
St. Ruald's (or St. Rumbold)	Goldsmith's Lane near Wilders old foundry	Southwest corner of Kine Croft, operating 1342; *thought to be possible 8th century*

The following map[26] from a detailed study that was carried out shows the extent of churches by 1300, but one can see the four that have been identified as having early "roots."

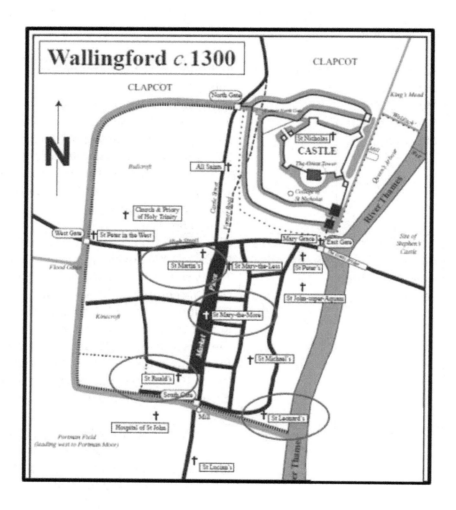

Could it be that any of the tunnels could relate to passages built for protection and access of clergy or other religious people during this time? We have already discussed the possible connection with St. Mary Le More. What about St. Leonard's? Could there be any connection here with stories about tunnels from Castle Priory under Thames Street into the town? While they are not the correct location, the stories might be related.

The old site of St. Martin's might be more interesting as this location coincides with the tunnels discussed at the Lamb Hotel and others around the area, and the thoughts that the High Street area shows an abundance of other stories (including a connection of a number of tunnels in this area). Could St. Martin's also be a point of connection back along the street to the door discovered during the renovations of KP Stationers in the Market Place? While the excavations carried out during the building of the new Waitrose revealed Saxon burials, there was no reported discovery of any doors, passages, crypts, or tunnels. However, we might consider that any such tunnels would by now be a good distance below the surface. As an example, at St. Aldates in Oxford where excavations found 12th, 13th and 15th century pottery, several discoveries were up to 6 metres below the surface.

There is no trace of any history on St. Peter's before it was designed and re-built in 1763, after the medieval building on this site had been destroyed during the Civil War in 1646 during the siege of Wallingford. If there was a medieval church, is it possible that there had also been older remains?

There is a crypt under the church[27] which apparently houses the remains of William Blackstone, who also had Castle Priory built. Yet there appears to be nothing written about earlier periods. Could the Blackstone crypt house any possible secrets? The location of St. Peter's relative to Calleva House, as well as to the locations of two stories about tunnels on High Street in houses that are directly opposite the entrance to Thames Street where St. Peter's is located. The Church stands on a rise in the land so there would be space underneath. But it's all speculation with almost no supporting facts.

As a last church-related observation, we might look at St Rumbold's church[28] which was also referred to as St. Ruald's. *"However, an early Anglo-Saxon settlement existed at Wallingford in the fifth and sixth centuries. This Mercian site gave rise to the foundation of St Rumbold's church as well as a substantial pagan cemetery in the south-western quadrant of the subsequent burh."*

If the church were located in what is now inside the earth works of the burh and the cemetery outside, to the south of St. John's Road[29], could that possibly mean they are connected in some way? Could this burial ground and the church actually go a bit further back to the end of the Roman era if the Romans had in fact settled Wallingford to any extent? There is certainly no trace of tunnels or anything, but it does, once again, support the development of early churches in the Wallingford area.

We might also have a wildly speculative thought. Given that the Romans had both a fear and respect for the dead and often created walls or trenches between cemeteries and churches, is it just possible that the ditches around the existing earthworks on the south of the Kine Croft marked the original boundary of the Roman settlement? Could the ditch have served both a defensive purpose, as part of some type of wall or even the existing earthworks, and a "barrier" between the settlement and the dead? This is highly speculative, and certainly not supported by the known archeology. Certainly, there are almost no reported tunnels in this area; however, there are several 20th century stories, about children who explored while playing in the brook around the Kine Croft and discovered what could have been tunnels. I received a story from one person, who reported *"Tunnels under Wallingford is true. I saw one before it was bricked up and another in the Kine Croft that was sectioned off before being filled."*

So, could there be a church connection to the tunnels that dates back to the pre-Norman period? Could these also in any way tie in with the stories about St. Mary's being built on the old Basilica (although when renovations were done in recent years and the floor was opened up no evidence was found - but did they actually excavate?)? Wallingford continued to expand, and many more churches were built which we will discuss later. Several of these have passed into history with neither a more modern church built over the top or any evidence of previous buildings below.

The Growth Era

In all probability, people who believe that there are tunnels under Wallingford would expect their construction and existence to coincide with Wallingford Castle. After all, there are typically good reasons supported by history that this time period marked the creation of tunnels for military reasons, including escape, communications, and supply, as well as for protection of people such as priests and clergy. It is a nice "romantic" notion and certainly a possibility. In this chapter, we will explore whether there is any evidence either at Wallingford or elsewhere that might support the theory of tunnels.

While the time frame from before the Roman invasion in AD 43, through to about 800 AD holds some small possibility of the creation of passages or tunnels, the next 600 years or so might hold more. There is an incredible richness of information around the development of Wallingford from this period, but for our discussions of tunnels we will avoid restating all of the material again. However, as part of the research there are a number of books, papers and essays that are strongly recommended as background reading for those who wish to delve more deeply into the "ideas and circumstantial evidence" around which this chapter focuses. Specifically recommended are:

- The website and everything associated with the Wallingford Museum.

- *"Wallingford: The Castle and the Town in Context,"* edited by K. S. B. Keats-Rohan, Neil Christie, David Roffe. BAR British Series 621, 2015
- *"Transforming Townscapes: From burh to borough. The archeology of Wallingford AD 800–1400,"* by Neil Christie and Oliver Creighton. Kindle Books
- *"Wallingford in Domesday Book and beyond, The Origins of the Borough of Wallingford: Archaeological and Historical Perspectives,"* edited by K. S. B. Keats-Rohan and D. R Roffe. British Archaeological Reports, British Series 494, 2009, 27-51.

There are also a number of references throughout the text and in the endnotes, to other sources; interested readers will discover that the history of Wallingford continues to evolve so that some earlier beliefs have since been modified or changed. As mentioned earlier, the challenges include the emergence of new facts as well as the interpretation of these facts. To try and create any hypothesis, especially based only on circumstantial evidence that tunnels existed, the easiest way is to provide an overview of key time periods and identify possibilities for the creation of such access routes.

Pre-Norman Wallingford

There is much discussion about the strength of evidence for the size of settlement in Wallingford, after the Romans and before the Normans. A large 6th century pagan cemetery found in Wallingford is one of the strongest indicators of the early presence of the Saxon newcomers. While there have been some archeological finds, building a history of this period, especially in terms of buildings or fortifications, is a challenge. However, once we reach the 9th century there was another invasion threat – this time from the Vikings.

King Alfred, the Saxon king of Wessex, defeated the initial incursions, but to defend his kingdom against further Viking attacks he built many fortified towns or 'burhs.' Wallingford was one of Alfred's "new towns", and the biggest. Around about 880, It was enclosed on three sides by earthworks, composed of earthen walls capped with a wooden palisade and surrounded by a wet moat. The river formed the fourth line of defence (the remains of the three sides can still be seen today around the Kine Croft and the Bull Croft). The original 9th century street layout is still largely unchanged. Tunnel believers might like to think that the creation of major earth works was a great opportunity to build tunnels. Who knows? There is not much evidence.

There are some interesting developments though. Recent excavations have started to make us question the location of the original earthworks in the southeast quadrant of the town. This raises the possibility that, at the time of construction, a tunnel in the Thames Street area might have been possible as an access route, maybe through some sort of postern gate, from inside the fortifications to outside on the Thames side of the earth mounds.

In reading through some of the documents identified above, a number of "milestones" and events seemed to jump out that can help our thinking. These include:

- Wallingford has been a continuous settlement for over 2,000 years although there is debate on many of the finer points of who, how, when, and how large.
- In 915 it was described as a "large burh – bigger than Oxford."
- The Danes apparently "burned down" the town in 1006 (although again there is debate as to whether they actually destroyed the town or did some lesser damage).
- Wallingford was one of the 'burhs' enumerated in the Burghal Hidage. By the time of 'Edward the Confessor', it was already a royal borough, and may have been occasionally a royal residence, as the king had 15 acres within the borough.
- There may have been buildings of some sort on the site of Wallingford Castle at this point, probably with Royal connection.
- Wigod held the honour of Wallingford and owned many properties;

he was Sherriff of Oxford, and "cup bearer to King Edward" but was also a supporter of William the Conqueror who, after the successful invasion visited Wigod at Wallingford.

- The property that the Castle was constructed on, was already owned by the King.
- In 1067 construction began on Wallingford Castle; in 1071 it received its first prisoners (this timing might suggest there was some level of fortifications including a jail or dungeon prior to the start of building).

So, before we even get to the point of the start of major construction work on Wallingford Castle, we might surmise that an advanced settlement, including some level of larger buildings, existed. We might even conclude that this included early buildings on the site of the castle, including a place to keep prisoners. The construction, updates, additions, and renovations of Wallingford Castle took place over an extended period of time, which offers plenty of possibilities for the creation of tunnels. Interwoven with this activity was the use of the Castle by royalty and high-ranking officials, including church members. Many of these may have wanted to gain access without being seen. So, there is certainly room for speculation that tunnels may have been part of this period (maybe even building on or expanding some minor ones that previously existed, related to early churches or even earlier). To explore this further, we can look at the churches in the 11th century, in and around the time of the Norman invasion.

Churches in the mid 11th century

There had been a gradual increase in church-building, as mentioned in an earlier chapter, with some of them possibly built as early as 400 but with a renewed development starting around 600 with St. Augustine. Earlier it was identified that maybe St. Mary Le More and St. Leonard's, which still stand, could have originated in much earlier times. Added to these were the now disappeared St. Ruald's (or St. Rumbold) and St. Martins, which might have been candidates for some type of tunnel. We can now look at the other churches and see if there might be any links here.

In the table, C1 represents the earliest date (i.e., century) of any mention or speculative origin and C2 represents a reference supported by some level of professional research.

Name	Location	C1	C2	Detail
Holy Trinity (Church and Priory)	High Street N	8	11	It is thought to have been established by Paul de Caen of St Albans (Abbott 1077 – 93), who was also responsible for building St. Albans Abbey. May have had Saxon origins.
St. Nicholas	Inside Castle	8	13	Founded as a chapel after Castle built linked to All Saints / All Hallows reflecting Royal alignment. Site may have been a previous chapel from the 8th century, possibly aligned with St. Mary's.
All Saints / All Hallows	Outside the castle – off Castle Street		11	Before 1101 had been granted by Miles Crispin (died 1107) to St. Nicholas within the castle. Mentioned in a patent of 1200, Destroyed in Civil War 1641–1647; graveyard remains on east side of Castle St.
St. Peter's (in the East)	St. Peter St.	11	17	Maybe built by Robert D'Oilly, (died 1091). 1374: amalgamated with St. Michael and St. Mary the Less. Original church in ruins after 1641 or 1642; rebuilt 1769, united with St. Mary-Le-More declared redundant 1971.
St. Lucians (or St. Lucien's)	South, Reading Road		12	Just behind almshouses. Given by King Henry 1 (1068–1135) to monastery of St. Frideswide

Name	Location	C1	C2	Detail
				(now Christ Church), Oxford. By 1291 granted to St. Leonard's Church.
St. Michael's	Cattle Market car park		13	Existed 1271. Parochial church, 1374 united with St. Peters, near Lower Wharf, slightly to north of St. Leonard's.
St. Peter in the West	High Street / St. Georges St.		13	Northwest corner of Kine Croft, built before 1271
St. Mary-the-Less (or Minor)	St. Mary's St. (Lower)		14	Parochial church; 1374 united with St. Peters; building was in ruins; stood opposite what was The Bear.
St. John-super-Aquam	Off Thames St. Nr. River	10	11	Northwest of Castle Priory; belonged to Holy Trinity. Mentioned as "in 1086 possibly belonging to Roger the Priest."

Holy Trinity church is interesting if it does have Saxon origins as it lies in the area of the later construction of the Priory. It is also in the area around Flint House / Bull Croft. Artist's depictions of the church and priory show a large collection of buildings with a central open space. It might be possible that the foundation of Flint House was part of one of these original buildings that extended from High Street back into the Bull Croft. If this was the case, the potential of an early tunnel connecting this church to other areas might increase.

While many associate St. Nicholas with the post conquest period, there are some who are open to the idea that a chapel existed prior to this date – possibly associated with St. Mary's. Certainly, once again, if this idea has any validity, it might suggest the existence of some hidden access connection. By the late 1070s, Robert d'Oyley had founded the college of St. Nicholas within the castle precincts and a Benedictine Priory in

Wallingford town (he apparently supported many religious buildings after his "conversion" caused by a dream). The Priory again would have been an addition to the church of Holy Trinity. This connection between the creation of the college, the chapel (possibly built on pre-existing Saxon remains), the Church of St. Nicholas and the Priory holds interesting potential for hidden access routes once again. The later development and updating of the chapel in 1278, as a chantry by Edmund, Earl of Cornwall, increased its size and role.

All Saints or All Hallows, although in no case dated back to Saxon times, appears to have existed at a location quite close to the Castle and was the church for a large parish that extended north into the area called Clapcot. It also seems to have been considered the royal "chapel" prior to the development of the chapel within the Castle. *"The charters of King John show that there were then two royal prebendal chapels at Wallingford; one of which is described as 'our chapel of Wallingford to wit the church of All Saints'; whilst there are several later references to prebends in 'our chapel within the castle.' The last of these is of the year 1214, when William de London received the king's letters of presentation to the prebend which had been held by Master William de Pottern, 'in the chapel of the Lord the King in the castle of Wallingford[30]."* Had this church been the one of Royal favour, it is not too unrealistic to believe that there might be access tunnels to the Castle from the location on Castle Street (at the location of the current graveyard on the east side of the street where a tunnel from the former Lamb Hotel is rumoured to run).

St. Peter's (in the East) is again an interesting site. It again might have origins in the 11th century or possibly earlier. It was located by the East gate and again recent archeological work on the river side of the property has revealed some interesting possibilities of remains beneath the foundations. It is also believed to have a crypt. This, connected to its proximity to Calleva House or the property on that site at the time, as well as High Street generally, makes it an interesting possibility. As we will discuss later, there are also possible connections with this location and the second siege of Wallingford by King Stephen.

If King Henry I (1068–1135) gave St. Lucians to the monastery of St. Frideswide, it must have been at some time during his reign – thus it is likely to have been built before then. Its location on Reading Road would appear to have been outside the burh boundaries but its dating supports the discussion of churches being plentiful in the area in the 11th century. (Its' location would also be subject to some recent thinking about where the earth fortification actually ran. Was the St. Lucians inside or outside?)

St. Michael's, which was located in what is now a car park, has also been subject to some of the archeological explorations that looked at an alternative location for the earthworks and outer boundaries of the burh. It could have been part of some Thames Street connections but again is a good "marker" for the number of churches.

St. Peter in the West, located at the corner of High Street and St. George's Road (now the location of the Cross Keys pub), would not appear to have been the subject of any discussion, although being along the road from St. Nicholas, the Priory (as well as Flint House / Stone Hall sites) could possibly have some linkages there; it is possible that the location might even be near to (or the location of) Stone Hall, which dates back to 1550. Given that it appears to have been in place before 1271, it likely was built after the earthworks in the Kine Croft were completed. Archeological work at the Cross Keys has revealed nothing about a possible church.

St. Mary the Less (or Mary the Minor) was located at the northern end of St. Mary's Street in the vicinity of High Street. This location is again interesting, although there is no specific dating of church foundations; however, renovations to create the Dolphin pub's car park, as well as some in the cellars of older properties near High Street, both found skeletons suggesting possibly a place of burial or cemetery. The proximity of this church to more stories of tunnels might again hold some interest.

St. John-super-Aquam was apparently located on the East side of Wallingford between the river and Thames Street, north of Castle Priory.

David Roffe offers that it probably existed in 1086 and discusses the possibility of it having been built in the late Saxon period. According to the British History website, *"The church of St. John-upon-the-water was in Thames Street, near the river. It belonged to the priory of Holy Trinity from 1160."* St. Michael's was also part of Holy Trinity at this time. Its location adjacent to St. Peters might hold some interest. There seem to be archaeological discoveries related to this church. There is also mention of a St. Mary de Stallis Church by Keats-Rohan in *"Most Securely Fortified: Wallingford Castle 1071–1540,"* but there appears no other mention of this name.

Finally, there were two chapels mentioned in Wallingford (although it is probable that the building originally located within the Castle had started out as a chapel also).

Name	Location	C1	C2	Detail
St. Mary of Grace Chapel	High St.		16	Wallingford bridge; destroyed in siege of 1646.
St. John the Baptist Chapel	Outside south gate;		13	Henry III granted letters of protection 1224. Aligned with Hospital of St. John.

So, what part might churches have played in the possibility of tunnels in the late Saxon and early Norman period. Here are a few thoughts:

- Churches were well established by this period and several current churches appear to be built on the foundations of older buildings.
- There was strong connection between royalty and certain churches, including both before and after Wallingford Castle was built.
- The church of St. Nicholas, which was later expanded and became part of the Priory was "ecclesiastically" connected to several other churches in Wallingford.
- The locations of certain churches appear to be possibly coincident

with tunnel stories.

- There was a "push – pull" of power between the church and royalty, which may have contributed to a desire for some level of secrecy.
- There are no specific stories of tunnels or even major crypts below any of the Wallingford churches having been seen or found.
- The locations of several of the churches do create possibilities of reasons for and / or the existence of passages.

Whether there were tunnels that evolved from churches and / or became part of a network of possible connections beneath Wallingford remains unproven, but the potential for such passages at the time of the Castle forms part of the bridge between speculation and possibility.

Evolution of Wallingford Castle

Construction of the new Castle was started on the northwest corner of the site;[31] according to the Castles, Forts, Battle's website, *"The Domesday Book (1086) recorded that 'eight sites (haguae) were destroyed for [construction of] the castle' which included a number of high-status Saxon residences and also involved disruption to part of the street grid (although not the main north/south and east/west thoroughfares). The builder of this new castle was Robert d'Oyley (or d'Oilly), a Norman Knight who had fought at the Battle of Hastings (1066) and who has built numerous other fortifications throughout the area including Oxford Castle."* It was not unusual for the building of a castle to require "appropriation" of local land but given the limited number of sites (located on the northwest area around Castle Street), it does suggest some level of mature development in Wallingford. So, let's stop and check our facts:

1. High-ranking individuals owned property, visited and / or lived in Wallingford.
2. Wallingford was a well established settlement by 1067.
3. The main part of settlement seems to have been to the south of the Castle.

4. It appears that the southeast quadrant of the town was most populated.
5. There appear to have been several established properties on both sides of High Street.
6. They may have been some previous properties on the site of the Castle.
7. These may have included a jail or dungeons.
8. The builder of Wallingford Castle also built Oxford Castle.

We can add to this list the possible fact that more than a few existing landowners and political figures might have been upset and held grudges against William. Although he "won", and people surrendered, human nature doesn't change and people "see where the wind is blowing and go with the flow." The following comment sums things up well:

> *William took all the land and important jobs in the Government and Church away from the Saxons and divided it up amongst his Norman friends. He built castles to make the English feel so scared that they would not dare even to think about causing trouble. By 1085, William had a shortage of money and also many Normans had begun to disagree amongst themselves over the land they had been given as a reward for helping conquer England. William wanted to settle these disputes once and for all. Thus, William decided to order a survey. The survey would list all the land in England. It would list who was looking after each area, what lands they had, and which other people lived there. Importantly, the survey would find out how much tax-money William could get from this land.*

Keats-Rohan and David Roffe's paper also provides some interesting analysis of who owned which property at this time. As stated, Wallingford appears to have been an important place and landowners included the King, the Bishop of Winchester (owning property including on the north side of High Street, one of which is The George Hotel); the Bishop of Lincoln (owning property in the Market Place); Hugh de Bolbec (property in St. Mary's Street); William FitzCorbucion (property somewhere in Holy Trinity Parish), and Nigel d'Aubigny (property in St. Mary Le More parish).

"Transforming Townscapes" (Section 5.8, Summary) provides a great foundation for discussing "possibilities" based on the five phases of Castle activity:

1. Pre 1070: the possible existence of a Royal Hall cited in the northeast corner of the original burh ("...sealed by the Norman Castle."). This might have dated from as early as the 9th or 10th century).
2. c. 1067–1071: the creation of the initial Norman fortification, a motte and single bailey with timber defences.
3. c. 1100s: upgrade from timber to stone and the addition of a "middle" bailey.
4. c. 1200s: upgrades to create a "show castle" (residence, rather than military bias).
5. c. 1600s: re-fortification and use during the English Civil War.

Could it also be that the Castle was "reconstructed" starting in 1067 based on earlier buildings? Keats-Rohan seems to think so: *"At Wallingford it used the northern rampart of the Saxon burh, situated in the north-east quadrant of the town, an area that gives every indication of having been an élite site associated with a royal hall and a 'garrison' of the armed retainers of both Edward the Confessor and Harold Godwinson, earl of Wessex and king of England. As such, it may have contained buildings, including a church, that could be incorporated or adapted into the new castle, or anyway affect the layout of the new castle."*

In this case, there might have been existing passages created between some of the buildings. If there were buildings on the Castle site, is it possible that there were already connections between this location and places in the town. Is it possible that, as part of the buildings on site, there was already some type of dungeon or jail – especially given the importance of Wallingford? Where might these have connected to? The choices would be churches or private residences. The problem with this scenario is that any tunnels would be deep under the ground and would probably have been further "buried" by the start of construction on the Norman castle, even had they been incorporated in some way.

1066	William the Conqueror invades England; October 14th: Battle of Hastings. December: Wigod welcomes William to Wallingford; the Archbishop of Canterbury and others "submit to William at Wallingford"; Earls Edwin, Morcar and Waltheof and the Archbishop of York surrender; Robert D'Oilly (or D'Oyley), favourite of William marries Wigod's daughter.
1067	William demands D'Oilly to build Wallingford Castle
1071	Castle motte and bailey completed; first prisoner brought to castle
1077	Wallingford Priory established by Abbot of St. Albans, (in what is now the Bull Croft)

So, what about the early period? Given the arrival of prisoners in Wallingford in 1071 there must have been a gaol at this time (which tends to be supported by Keats-Rohan). If this is the case, it is hard to see what new tunnels may have been created – but what about incorporation of earlier tunnels related to the gaol? Could this also have been a time when some early access was being provided between any churches and the Castle? The possibilities include All Saints / All Hallows on Castle Street, especially as this was seen as the "Royal Church" at this time. What about the possibility of tunnels between what is now The George (or that area) being property that appears to have been owned by the Church (Bishop of Winchester), and either the "old" chapel in the Castle or even St. Nicholas College?

There could be other possibilities, but this era of construction suggests a "first phase," focused on re-affirming the king's presence in

Wallingford rather than building an elaborate place of residence. However, Wallingford continued to grow; *"The Domesday book says there are 491 houses in Wallingford, and 22 Frenchmen living in the town, amongst about 3000 residents in total."* While there is debate over the numbers, it would indicate that a number of people probably having "developing" business with the Castle were located outside its boundaries and many of these were in the High Street area. Might this have included troops stationed at the Castle, but living outside the fortifications?

Could it be that in the period between 1071 and the later renovations attributed to Brian FitzCount, there was a level of on-going construction (that might have included developing methods of access between properties in the town and the Castle)? This continuity of castle development seems to be borne out by Keats-Rohan again, who states that there were several changes made before 1139: *"It is suggested here that the great tower was built on the initiative of Henry I (reigned from 1100–1135) overseen by constable Brien fitzCount, between 1113 and 1135. It may have been one of a number of enmotted keeps built between 1100 and 1150, and like many of them could have started as a small pre-Conquest stone tower or a noble residence that was further enhanced and fortified by the addition of a motte, a move that on completion would have fixed the final layout of the inner bailey."* However, arriving at 1139 we see the following:

1139	Brien FitzCount fortifies the castle; Stephen lays siege to castle, builds two counter castles which are destroyed.
1141	Stephen again lays siege to the castle (Wallingford Bridge is mentioned).
1142	Stephen lays siege again to the castle (from his castle built in Crowmarsh).
1146	Stephen again attacks Wallingford.
1152	Stephen again attacks the castle, takes Wallingford Bridge, and builds two counter castles with a wooden tower on one.
1153	Henry attacks the counter castle and builds earthworks around it; captures the bridge turret; truce eventually signed; Crowmarsh Castle is destroyed.

This period is therefore of interest in terms of both the investment being made in expanding and improving the Castle and the military activities.

By 1139, England had descended into civil war over the succession to the English crown. Henry I, who died in 1135, left only a daughter, Matilda, as his heir. Henry's supporters (the barons) had sworn loyalty to Matilda during the king's lifetime, but at his death they switched allegiance to her cousin, Stephen of Blois. Matilda's half-brother – Robert, Earl of Gloucester – declared his support for her and civil war was inevitable.

Matilda's support centred around Gloucestershire but also included much of southwest England and southern Wales. Although Brian FitzCount held Wallingford Castle and was one of her supporters, the Castle was at the edge of her support. Stephen placed Wallingford Castle under siege in 1139–1140 (the first siege) and built two counter castles, one of which was around St Peter's Church (although this is not clear based on Bradbury (1998), who suggests one castle was outside the west gate and another over the bridge in Crowmarsh). The second siege was in 1146 and, finally, before a treaty was negotiated, the third siege in 1152–53. In both the second and third sieges, it appears that Stephen's counter castles and other defences were based across the Thames in the riverside meadows (or thereabouts) in Crowmarsh[32].

There are several interesting points from this time period. First, Keats-Rohan makes a point about *"...the extraordinary role played by Wallingford in the civil war of Stephen's reign, when castle and town spent many years between 1139 and 1152 under increasingly close siege. The castle garrison could not have held out so considerably longer than any other castle of the time had it not both controlled the town gates and had the support of the townsmen."* Does this reference to "support of the townsmen" in any way suggest that there may have been access tunnels from outside the defences to inside so that support could be provided even though the Castle was under siege? However, there is also a negative connotation in that – if the Castle were successfully placed under siege, such that on the third occasion they agreed to a "proud surrender" – how would they have reached this condition, if there were access tunnels to allow for re-provisioning?

The second point relates to the location of the counter-castles in Crowmarsh; does this possibility add any credence to the stories of tunnels "under the river to Crowmarsh" or indeed those to Crowmarsh Hill or the French Meadows area of Howbery? It may be a bit of a stretch, but historic accounts indicate that Stephen focused significant resources to gain the Castle. Could this have included trying to tunnel in? Also, if, by any small chance, one of the counter castles was on the west side of the river by St. Peters, might this have also led to a tunnel?

After the Treaty of Wallingford was signed in 1153, Henry, who went on the become Henry II, was recognized as the rightful heir to the throne. Soon after, in 1155, he granted Wallingford its Charter. Between 1190 and 1193, the Castle changes hands a few times. 'Richard I' reined from 1189 to 1199, at which time his brother John became king. The 11th century was also the time of the Crusades, and this will have had an impact on relationships between the Catholic church and the monarchy, in particular the initial financial burden of the First Crusade (1096–1099). For example, William II's brother, Robert Curthose, Duke of Normandy, who took part in the First Crusade, was said to have pledged the Duchy of Normandy as surety for a 10,000-mark loan that his brother gave him to fund his crusading effort. To raise this money, William II, in turn, levied a crusading tax of 4 shillings to the hide on his kingdom, an imposition so severe that monks were said to have been forced to melt down sacred ornaments to pay for it.

When John became king there was a level of unrest; bishops had been exiled and knights taken prisoner, and John was concerned about the safety at Wallingford Castle. So, in 1215, another set of improvements was made to the Castle to "repair the moats and strengthen the fortifications." There seem to have been continual changes, improvements, and additions throughout the 13th century, during which time the Castle changed hands many times and may have been widely used by royalty. In 1278, the collegiate chapel of St. Nicholas, within the castle, was endowed (not founded) for the souls of his father and mother, of King Henry his uncle and of King Edward, granting it lands for the maintenance of a master, six chaplains, six clerks and four acolytes. This indicates the continued importance of the Church as an active part of Castle life.

In the 14th century, the Castle continued in active use (but was starting to become expensive to maintain: *"The large sums expended in keeping the buildings in repair at this period appear in an inquest of 1308."* Again, activity in the Castle involved changes of custodian and ownership; one of these events[33] provides a possible insight into the existence of a postern gate (maybe leading to an access tunnel?) used to gain entry to the Castle in 1322. *"The plan with regard to the Tower failed, but the conspirators, led by one Roger de Wauton, won over the governor of Wallingford, who admitted them by a postern gate near the river, and thus they got possession of the castle."*

Many of these changes resulted in further expenditures on the Castle. After the 1361 marriage of the Black Prince to the "Fair Maid of Kent" (his cousin Joan, the daughter of Edmund Earl of Kent), the princess made Wallingford Castle her chief residence. *"Considerable building works were undertaken at this period, probably in consequence of the princess's residence there, and in 1364 carpenters, masons and other workmen were being impressed for the repair of the castle."* After she became a widow, the expenses continued: *"She was frequently in residence at the castle, and many building works were undertaken there during her widowhood from 1378 onwards."* It appears that the financial burden of the Castle was increasing. *"The inquiry into the financial burdens on the honour (of Wallingford), undertaken in 1384, was resumed, and in 1387 it was reported that the revenues of Wallingford Castle were so diminished that the castle could not be supported without provision for its succour."*

Use of the Castle continued in the 15th century: *"On 30 June 1415 Henry V gave his mother licence to reside in any of his castles of Windsor, Wallingford, Berkhampstead, or Hertford while the king was on his present voyage beyond the sea. On his marriage with Katherine of France the castle and honour of Wallingford formed part of her dower, and she held it till her death in 1437. Considerable repairs were undertaken in 1424, with a view of making the castle more fit for the queen's residence, and in 1428 it was appointed as a summer residence for the young king Henry VI."* Again, as we can see, maintenance expenses continued.

Wallingford remained important as the major prison for Berkshire; *"A state prison was also enduring; in 1438 a new prison was constructed with a hall, kitchen and chambers for the gaolers; although its exact location is unknown (a 1555 survey recorded two prisons 'within the keep'). Furthermore, during the political struggles in 1450 the castle was again heavily fortified and repaired by William de la Pole, constable since 1434, who 'stuffed it with guns, gunpowder and other material of war'."* By 1491, Henry VIII had come to power and disagreements between King and the Church started in earnest.

The 16th century brought no more construction and the final days of the Castle as an active royal residence although it did serve as a prison for some time. *"In 1518 the court was in residence at Wallingford, and Pace, writing to Wolsey on 14 July, said that the king was at Wallingford, but that he was leaving for Bisham on the following day on account of the sickness. This is one of the last notices of the use of Wallingford Castle as a royal residence. Henry's visits were rare, and those of his successors rarer still."* In 1540 the castle and honour of Wallingford were separated from the duchy of Cornwall and annexed to the king's manor of Ewelme, which was erected into the honour of Ewelme, all the liberties and privileges of Wallingford Honour being transferred to it.

This may be connected to stories about "tunnels to Ewelme" which seems impractical because of the distance, but if the concept of a "route to Ewelme" gradually became a story about a tunnel, this might make sense. In 1547, King Henry VIII was succeeded by Edward VI; however, 1534 saw the Act of Supremacy declared making Catholicism a capital offence; the persecution of the church had started prior to this date and became a major issue. This once again may have some relationship to the further use, if not construction of, tunnels and passages as secret escape routes.

1524	Wallingford Priory dissolved and stones re-used.
1538	Wallingford Castle said to be in ruins.
1646	Wallingford Castle the only remaining Royalist stronghold in England – it withstood a siege for 12 weeks but surrendered after negotiation on July 27th to Sir Thomas Fairfax.
1652	November 18th: Cromwell ordered the destruction of Wallingford Castle.
1817	Castle site sold.

It is unlikely that any further activity at the Castle adds to our story of the creation of tunnels; indeed, at this point, with the widespread decay of the condition of the Church and the dissolution of the Priory, it is a time when tunnels, if they had been in place, would have also started to deteriorate. However, they might have been used for "uncontrolled" exploration as well as ecclesiastical hiding and escape. Had there been tunnels relating to the gaols, these may have continued in use – possibly if they included access points to the river which was used for transportation in some cases. Many of the local churches had also fallen into disrepair or been demolished by this period, so again tunnels relating to these, whilst they may have remained in place would have increasingly been covered up, collapsed, or filled with rubble from further re-building and development of the town.

Before we move on the "closing the loop" and looking for potential ways to connect stories to the various periods of construction and development in Wallingford, we will look at possible comparable situations across England. There are many other locations where tunnels have been uncovered, which may relate to Wallingford.

Tunnels and Passages Elsewhere

As many of the books and articles on Wallingford state, the Castle site is unique in that it has not been dug up or destroyed by any significant level of later development. For archeology that is good, but sadly it also means that there are limited actual ruins to see. Even archeology has some challenges in that the demolition, together with later landscaping has covered up and / or smoothed out some of the land works. Some of this had even occurred during the lifetime of the Castle, as was discussed earlier. Are there Roman remains buried deep down? Were there Saxon buildings beneath the existing Norman site? Did changes and alterations after 1071 cover up some aspects of earlier construction?

It is also likely that, if tunnels ever did exist, they were built either before or during the construction of the Castle up to about 1200. This probably means that they are, in most cases deeply buried under today's pastures, meadows, building and roads. The investigations that have taken place to date have not revealed any significant tunnels – so if they are buried deeply, are there other locations similar to Wallingford, where ruins of old castles or buildings are still standing and where tunnels have been found?

We talked about Roman era fortifications earlier, as these were sometimes used as the base for construction of either a Saxon or Norman fortification later. These would be the longest locations providing any level of continuity but there are few of them. However, before we go further, we can look at the English Heritage site[34] for a short context history.

- 900–200 BC: Hillforts. There are over 1200 hillforts in England; the earliest forts were probably built around 900 BC.
- 50–280 AD: Roman Forts (Phase 1). The Romans built forts and fortresses all over the country to provide secure accommodation for their troops. Earlier forts were defended by turf and timber ramparts, ditches, and wooden towers, although from the 2nd century AD many were rebuilt in stone.
- 280–400 AD: Roman Forts (Phase 2). The Romans, fearing attack, built a string of coastal defensive forts, referred to as the "Saxon Shore forts" along the south and east coasts, including Pevensey Castle, Portchester Castle and Richborough.
- 400–1000 AD: Not much castle building apart from the creation by Alfred of defensive burhs like Wallingford.
- 1000–1200: Norman castles. Starting after the invasion, the Normans built castles for the next 150 years, and "covered the country" with them, building around 1,000 in England and Wales. The 12th century saw the addition of keeps. In the late 12th and 13th centuries, castle defensive improvements were made and after that the focus was more on comfort.

These dates align well with what was seen at Wallingford. The research has been based on publicly available materials – articles, reports, websites etc. – and so has been taken at face value. There is probably considerable additional in-depth research that could be done by accessing local authority and other records. This material is presented in five main groups.

1. There appear to be at least three castles identified as Norman that pre-existed in some manner – possibly dating back to Saxon or Roman times. We might think of this as sites where tunnels could "bridge" into the Norman time period (maybe like Wallingford?).
2. The second group of six castles are identified in *"Wallingford: The*

Castle and the Town in Context" (Keats-Rohan, Christie, Roffe) as locations having been "built by William or with his approval."

3. The third group of five castles, come from the same period but do not appear as "officially sanctioned" Norman castles – even though historical research seems to place them in the same group as above.
4. There is a single location that is from the late Norman period but not included as a Norman castle as it was re-built at a later date.
5. The final locations discussed do not relate to Norman castles but to ancient tunnels under older towns and cities. These demonstrate how towns similar to Wallingford seem to have similar stories – but some of them have more specific "eyewitness" accounts.

Castles that are possibly pre-Norman

Two of these castles are mentioned by Historic England as being "good candidates" for tunnels – Dover and Pevensey. They also mention Carlisle and Farleigh and Hungerford, which we deal with later. For Dover Castle, they state, "*secret chambers and underground passage back to Medieval Times.*" So, lets start here.

Dover Castle

The origin of settlement on Castle Hill, where Dover Castle stands, may be in the pre-Roman Iron Age. Seventy years after the Roman invasion in AD 43, construction of a fort began at the mouth of the river Dour. The Romans also built an octagonal tower-like lighthouse (pharos) on Castle Hill around the same time. The pharos was later reused for the church of St Mary in Castro as a chapel and bell tower.

The church of St Mary in Castro dates to around AD 1000. Its exceptional size hints that it might have had a royal patron – Godwin, Earl of Wessex is one possibility. A cemetery discovered during archaeological excavations in 1962 indicated that a community lived nearby, perhaps in a fortified burh. So – an interesting comparison with the history of

Wallingford, not only for its possible links back to Roman or prior times, but also because it also suffered sieges and was updated and improved in later years for defensive purposes. According to English Heritage this include the creation of tunnels to assist in troop movements internally.

Dover Castle has a rich history of tunnels, but a key challenge is the degree to which these can be identified as being similar in any way to Wallingford. Although it is stated that there are "3 miles of tunnels" under Dover Castle, most of these were part of the wartime defences, starting with the Napoleonic Wars where seven tunnels were completed by 1803. However, the earliest date links to a possible comparison to Wallingford *"...you can't help yourself but venture down into the damp, dark winding Medieval tunnels, they were burrowed out under the castle, during the Siege of 1216[35]."* Another statement from a local Kent newspaper[36] tells us *"Between 1216–17 the castle was besieged by French forces. Tunnels were dug beneath the castle's great towers to undermine them."*

A further story[37] about actual excavations reads *"The first tunnels to be excavated date to 1217–1257 and are located at the old north entrance connecting an outwork and tower, built outside the defences, to the castle. Tunnels were also placed on the western side of the defences."* So, with these references we appear to have possible comparisons with a) Roman activity, b) tunnels built during a siege, and c) tunnels that have been excavated.

Pevensey Castle

The second Castle is Pevensey. Historic England says there are "2 dungeons and hidden passage." Pevensey also starts life as a Roman location although it appears to have been built in marshy land and accessed by a bridge. As far as the Medieval period is concerned, Sussex Archeology and Folklore states[38] that *"There are two dungeons under the castle, one reached by a spiral staircase and the other by a trapdoor. Whilst the last usage of these chambers was as dungeons, it is thought that their original purpose was for storage."* This is reinforced by Wikipedia, where it states

"A 'secret tunnel' exists at Pevensey Castle in East Sussex, although not open for public access. It links the keep with the former market square and is thought to be Norman in origin; it was reused during the Second World War." One of the dungeons is in fact an "oubliette" so there would have been just a trap door entrance on the top and no other way out.

There is also a story that appears to have started as part of tunnel folklore and was investigated. *"Local folklore links Pevensey Fort with a house in Westham, over 2 miles distant, called Priesthawes. A local man recalled having found a tunnel south-west of the western gateway. Mr. Lower (1853 p.276) in his excavations did indeed find a tunnel in the form of a drain 18 inches high and constructed from large stones. Running north-west to south-east, it would have missed both the fort and the village of Westham. This tunnel was investigated again by Manwaring-Baines (1967) who considered it to be a drain dating to Tudor times."* Clearly neither part of the tunnel that ran to the Castle, was in reality large enough to be a human passage. This demonstrates the type of stories that develop over time.

Lincoln Castle

The last Castle in this group is Lincoln. It appears that Lincoln also dates back to Roman times and that when a church was demolished it was found to have been built on the site of a Roman basilica; remains of the larger forum were also found. As the Roman Lincolnshire website explains: *"Mint Wall is one of the most significant but overlooked Roman remains in Britain. Tucked away around the back of the Castle Hotel, it is one of the largest pieces of freestanding Roman building wall to be seen in the country. The wall is the only surviving remnant of the Basilica – the large public hall which stood at the northern end of the forum and would have been central to the governance of the Colonia."*

Lincoln is also interesting related to the history of the basilica and its relationship to local churches. *"There are few attested late Roman Christian churches in Britain, and Lincoln has a claim to being the site of one. The archaeological evidence is not currently conclusive, but a series of churches excavated within the courtyard of the Roman forum may have originated in the 4th Century. The excavation of the Roman forum between 1972 and 1978 was enabled through the demolition of the church of St Paul in the Bail. That last church on the site was of Victorian date, itself a replacement for earlier Georgian and Medieval churches. The excavations revealed traces of even earlier churches in the sequence, and of possible physical connections to the Roman forum structure."* Could this be compared to St. Mary Le More in Wallingford?

Other Norman castles

These castles and the ones in the previous section all appear as castles that were part of the initial Norman building programme[39]. *"Of the 36 castles ordered to be built by William I, 20 were placed in the leading boroughs of each county, with Wallingford being among the very first. These were the 'castles of conquest', and they were initially about control, of both the people and the machinery of governance and the economy. Twelve of them were located in towns with Roman roots, and eight in English burhs, including Wallingford and Oxford. In each case the new castle adapted one or more of the existing ramparts or walls in the construction of one or more of its sides, usually in a corner position close to the river and with ready access to and control over the river bridge. The evidence of Domesday Book, collected during 1086, shows that in most cases a sizeable number of properties were destroyed to make way for the castle and its perimeter, evidence that these castles were intended to establish a secure and commanding position within the towns."* We know that in Wallingford only "eight hagae (enclosed burgage plots)" located on the east side, near what became the North Gate, were destroyed. However, in all other aspects Wallingford Castle would probably have been similar.

In order to give some context to the various stories about tunnels, we have updated the original map[40] to show where these castles were located. Each location discussed is marked with a triangle at the approximate location and where these were not originally included, the name has been added. We have also added locations where Norman castles appear to have also been added but were not identified in the original 36.

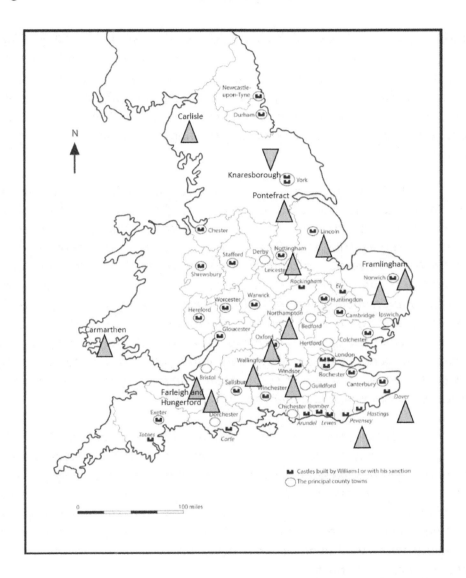

We have already dealt with the first three castles (and of course Wallingford). Now the next six, starting with Nottingham.

Nottingham Castle

Nottingham Castle was originally built as part of the initial Norman construction programme and functioned until destroyed in the Civil War. It was rebuilt as a duke's mansion in the 1670s. The mansion's medieval caves, however, survived the conflict, including the dungeon (where King David II of Scotland was reportedly held prisoner in 1346). These have recently been mapped using advanced 3D imagery to show the tunnels and dungeon.

Nottingham appears to have an interesting geology that supported the "easy" construction of caves and passages. This quote from Atlas Obscura[41] may sound familiar to those interested in Wallingford's possible tunnels. *"The Nottingham Caves Survey, a project by researchers at Nottingham University to digitally map the caves, has seen many local homeowners come forward to reveal that they too have caves leading off into the subterranean maze from their basements or tucked away in the corner of their garden. Some have been surprised to learn that their particular cave was previously unknown. As recently as January 2017, a group of students living on one of the main roads into the city, Mansfield Road, discovered a series of steps leading down from their cellar into a previously unknown void under the city streets."*

The commentary goes on to explain that they believe *"The caves were dug for many reasons – as workplaces, such as the medieval tannery, as (part of) homes, as secret passages and tunnels, such as those at Castle Rock; as storerooms, brewhouses, and public houses; as prisons and dungeons; and in more recent history, as air raid shelters during the Nottingham Blitz. Scattered across the city are small doors and gates, complete with rusty padlocks that cover access points into the greatly interconnected labyrinth."*

However. what about tunnels and the castle? A 2017 headline in the local paper[42] may give a clue: *"Secret tunnels connecting Nottingham Castle to city centre 'are a myth'."* This article seems clear, yet we find on the Ancient Pages website[43] a seeming researched and supported story that there are in fact tunnels under Nottingham Castle that pre-date its construction and relate to its original name of "Place of Caves." They sometimes served as a chapel, kilns for malt and pottery or tannery. It is interesting that these uses are similar to some of the archeology discovered at Wallingford. They also quote historically based use of tunnels in 1330 to access the Queen's bedroom by Edward III to arrest Mortimer, the lover of Queen Isabella who was taken to London and executed. This access tunnel can still be seen and visited. So, does Nottingham have any parallels for Wallingford?

Norwich Castle

Norwich is one of 48 castles mentioned in the Domesday survey of 1086 and was one of those initiated to establish the Norman presence. It sits on a pre-existing mound, where a king named Gungunt, Gungant or Gurgunt, who was said to have built the castle 'before Roman times', was buried. Excavations in the late 1970s discovered that the castle bailey was built over a Saxon cemetery. The construction, updating and improvements to the castle are quite similar to those in Wallingford. There are many stories published in various sources about tunnels, connected to Norwich as well as to many other locations in East Anglia[44]. There is another interesting parallel to Wallingford, in that there was a "Jewish Quarter" in what is now around the Lamb down the north side of High Street towards the river. The Normans introduced Jews to Norwich, and they also lived close to the castle.

Norwich apparently has the largest number of medieval undercrofts (crypts) in the country[45]. The oldest of these is in Wensum Lodge, Kings Street. Just a few feet below Norwich Magistrates' Court[46] stand the well-preserved remains of a Norman house; the house was discovered during excavations on the site in 1981 before the courts were built; there was no documentary evidence of the house. Built in about

1170, probably for the Cathedral priory, it was in ruins by the 13th century. The court building itself was built over the remains of the Norman house, (which now stands in its basement and can be viewed).

There are also plenty of stories about tunnels. *"From the remains of the Norman castle, three tunnels are said to lead to the now-demolished Elizabethan mansion of Boyland Hall at Morningthorpe many miles to the east, to Kenninghall Place to the south-west, and to the scant remains of the priory that once stood on the site of Old Buckenham Castle just 1.5 miles north."* [47]

The Hidden East Anglia website talks about *"...a whole host of legendary tunnels under Norwich leading from the Castle."* The stories explain that one tunnel goes to the Guildhall, near the market-place, erected 1407 on the site of the old tollhouse. (This still has a 14th century vault below it that was the crypt and prison of the former building.) A second tunnel heads from the castle for Carrow Priory, a 12th century Benedictine nunnery on the outskirts of Norwich, now incorporated into a residence. A third tunnel from the castle runs to the Norman cathedral to the northeast, begun in 1096 by Bishop Herbert de Losinga, and finally consecrated in 1101.

This site also has a story about a tunnel that starts at the cathedral, running for about 9 miles to the ruins of St. Benet's Abbey. A much shorter tunnel, allegedly used by monks, was said to run from the cathedral to Samson & Hercules House. *"The cathedral and St. Gregory's church are two destinations of passages believed to originate beneath the 16th century Augustine Steward House in Tombland. There is certainly an undercroft beneath the House which extends beneath the pavement in the direction of the cathedral, and people have spoken of blocked-up tunnel entrances."*

So, there are some common denominators between Wallingford and Norwich: church, castle, and priory linkages with hidden tunnels for monks. Norwich was the county gaol and there is still a prisoner's tunnel. But once again there's no clear evidence of actual tunnels other than individual crypts and access passages. There have been some investigations of tunnels under Castle Meadows, supposed to link to the castle, but these have been professionally discounted.

Probably the most likely proof might come from a report in Archeology Data Services: *"In the 1980s work began on construction of the vast underground Castle Mall shopping centre in Norwich. The associated archaeological excavation was one of the largest of its kind in northern Europe, designed to investigate not only the castle bailey but also pre-Conquest settlement and, for the post-Conquest period, areas of the surrounding medieval city. The report describes evidence for late Saxon streets, houses and graveyards; the developing fortifications of an urban castle established before 1100; gradual encroachment by the townspeople into the castle precinct after the 13th century; documentation relating to the ownership and development of properties within the Castle Fee."* But they found no tunnels or passages.

Windsor Castle

Obviously, a favourite and one of the few castles from this period both maintained and in use. This should provide some unique insights, then, to possible comparison with Wallingford. The original castle was built in the 11th century after the Norman invasion of England by William the Conqueror. Since the time of Henry I, who was the first monarch to actually use the castle, it has been used by the reigning monarch and is the longest-occupied palace in Europe. Windsor Castle was strategically important because of its proximity to both London and the River Thames.

One of most topical and well publicized stories about tunnels was part of a BBC documentary. This quote from *The Sun* newspaper provides a good summary: *"The Queen's Palaces delved into the history of Windsor, which was built in the 11th century, and is still one of the 93-year-old's official residences. Back in the 1000s, secret passageways and escape routes were a necessity, and one was included by the architects of the royal residence, which leads out onto the street. Presenter Fiona Bruce revealed the hidden passageway for the first time on camera, saying you can still find evidence of the castle's 'war like origins' if 'you know where to look'. Beneath the door is a set of impressive stone steps, which haven't changed since they were built. Fiona said: 'If you're a soldier in Windsor Castle under siege you need a way to get out'. And this is the secret passage."* From the video, this tunnel looked exceptionally large.

We do know that Windsor Castle had dungeons as these were used as air raid shelters by royalty when they were there during the Second World War. We also know there were vaults under the castle as that is where the Crown Jewels were hidden during the war.

On the British History website there is talk of an access tunnel: *"...a sallyport into the old south ditch. This is now entered through the floor of one of the southern rooms and consists of a passage about 5 ft. wide with pointed head, lined with excellent masonry. Where it passes under the walls it is spanned by round-headed arches, which also contract the passage to 3½ ft. Beyond the passage the sallyport becomes a long tunnel with a descending floor, cut through the solid chalk. Its outlet in the ditch is now blocked and buried."*

British History Online also talks of several passages related to the vault and royal burial crypts below ground as well as those linking the chapel and the clergy quarters. There are other references: *"The main floor of the Clewer tower has a doorway on the south communicating with a mural chamber, through the floor of which access can now be had to a postern passage and sallyport, constructed in the thickness of the curtain wall at its building. The passage is 6 ft. wide and filled with a descending flight of forty chalk and stone steps, covered by a sloping barrel vault of chalk blocks, plastered. The sides of the stair are of coursed chalk blocks. At the stair foot the passage turns at a right angle and continues down into the ditch, but its lower end and opening are blocked."* Does this refer to the same passage as the documentary?

Once again, we have similarities to Wallingford but nothing about any large amounts of tunnels leading out of the Castle itself. (Although there was a story of a tunnel uncovered in the City of Windsor that no one seemed to know what it was for or where it went. When first reported it was denied that it went to the castle and was still "under investigation." No follow-up story was found. This would probably be due to the reality of Windsor being an active royal residence as there are not going to be many stories made public about access.)

Bristol Castle

Bristol has again a similar background to Wallingford, starting as a motte and bailey constructed of wood. Stephen, who had laid siege at Wallingford, was captured in 1141, and was imprisoned in Bristol Castle until Robert of Gloucester was also captured and an exchange of prisoners was made. Changes and additions were made over the years and Bristol became one of the most important royal castles in the country. Henry III, (1207–1272), who was educated in Bristol in his youth, spent lavishly on it, adding a barbican before the main west gate, a gate tower, and magnificent great hall.

Little remains of the castle today but there are some suggestions that tunnels did exist. Today, Castle Park occupies the area where the castle existed. The castle occupied the whole of the eastern end of the park, just east of St. Peter's Church to Lower Castle Street. By the 16th century the castle was in bad shape and Oliver Cromwell decreed its destruction in 1655, a process which was completed within a fortnight. Some of the tunnels date back to the 12th century when Bristol was the centre for wine imports.

The first is a story supported by cellars and passages that apparently exist under the city. Bristol was a major centre of wine importation in the 12th century. One example is the entrance to two wine cellars beneath High Street, that were used to store wine and other imports brought to Bristol via the River Avon. Peter Fleming, who is a professor of history at the University of the West of England, was quoted in *Bristol Live*[48], saying *"I don't think we know precisely when they were built but we believe it was some time during the 14th or 15th century. One of the cellars, would have been used to keep barrels, while the other would have served as a showroom. I have been down there and been inside and I have seen the vaults. Members of the public aren't normally allowed down because the entrance is very narrow, and I don't think some people would be able to make it down."* The article in *Bristol Live* goes on to say, *"Many of these underground tunnels were inter-linked, making it possible to walk from Corn Street under the centre, to Castle Park."*

A second story is about a quite different tunnel. A hidden network of pitch-black tunnels under Bristol's Castle Park that run under the ruins of the 11th century castle were explored by two kayakers armed with cameras. The passages are situated under the ruins of the castle that was built in the later part of the 11th century. This "waterway" is also discussed in the book, "Secret Underground Bristol", written by Sally Watson; she invites the reader to look over the edge of the river wall by the ambulance station near Castle Park to see an entrance to the moat that once went around the Castle. (Sally studied archaeology at the University of Bristol and spent a lot of time exploring the city's underground history, much of which is now not accessible to the public.)

There was also a sally port, one of the hidden entryways to the old Norman keep of Bristol Castle, which was discovered in 1991. Accessed via an underground tunnel, it once allowed goods and people to enter and leave the building undetected. There is also a video of "never before seen footage" of a labyrinth of tunnels dating back to the 1300s that were apparently built to supply fresh water for the monks. Bristol also has a Facebook page tied in with "Bristol Then and Now" where there continue to be extensive discussions about tunnels under the city. However, once again there is almost no archeological evidence to demonstrate actual tunnels under the castle that led outside.

Oxford Castle

From a Wallingford perspective this is a good comparison candidate. The first buildings were constructed by Robert D'Oyley who also built Wallingford Castle. It was also built adjacent to the river which formed part of the fortifications. Most of the original moated, wooden motte-and-bailey castle was replaced in stone in the late 12th or early 13th century. In the 14th century the military value of the castle diminished, and the site became used primarily for county administration and as a prison. The surviving rectangular St. George's Tower is now believed to pre-date the remainder of the castle and be a watch tower associated with the original Saxon west gate of the city.

Most of the castle was destroyed in the English Civil War and by the 18th century the remaining buildings had become Oxford's local prison. The medieval remains of the castle, including the motte and St. George's Tower and crypt, are Grade I listed buildings and a Scheduled Monument, and can be visited as a tourist attraction. Looking at Oxford, there may be four areas of interest related to Wallingford:

- What underground areas are there in the castle?
- Are there passages or tunnels from the castle to elsewhere?
- Is there any connection between the castle and churches?
- Are there any other stories about Oxford tunnels that may be relevant?

Like Wallingford, inside the walls of the castle the buildings included a chapel with a crypt attached to St. Georges Tower, which may be on the site of a previous church. The chapel originally had a nave, chancel, and an apsidal sanctuary. In 1074, D'Oyley (and Roger d'Ivry) had endowed a chapel with a college of priests, with a dedication to Saint George.

The crypt of this chapel[49] still survives, and therein is part of a challenge. It is now in a new location, within the castle, having been moved and reconstructed from its original materials in 1794 and this is what visitors see. The original materials  provide some level of comparison and continuity with the original and what might be found elsewhere. There are four original pillars still here (as seen in the picture) that were built by expert craftsmen, by hand in 1074.

There is also a design similarity to the stairs under the keep. Oxford Castle is described as having, *"The ten-sided stone shell keep, 58 feet, constructed in the 13th century to replace an earlier wooden structure, closely resembled those of Tonbridge and Arundel Castles. The keep enclosed a number of buildings, leaving an inner courtyard only 22 feet across. Within the keep, stairs led 20 feet down to an underground 12 feet wide stone chamber, with an Early English hexagonal vault and a 54 foot-deep well providing water in the event of siege."*

Apart from the specific mentions of the crypt there is no other definitive information about tunnels under or connecting with the castle. However, there are many stories like those in Wallingford. There is a legend about an underground passage that led into the crypt. Henry II apparently used the tunnel when he visited Oxford. He passed through the tunnel to avoid his Queen while seeing his mistress.

There was also a church built close to the castle, named St. Peter-le-Bailey: *"The church of St. Peter at the Castle was also known as St. Peter-in-the-West or St. Peter-le-Bailey."* The church was granted to St. Frideswide's Priory in 1122, the same as St. Lucians in Wallingford. The Church has existed in or near the area now known as Bonn Square, since the 12th century. The suffix "le-Bailey" was due to its position close to Oxford Castle. This also distinguished it from Oxford's other church dedicated to St. Peter, namely St. Peter-in-the-East, near the original east gate of the city, now the library of St. Edmund Hall. Since the inception of the parish, there have been three different church buildings. The first church was built in the 12th century.

There are also stories about another possibly related church, St. Peter-in-the-East. Underneath St. Peter-in-the-East (now St. Edmund Hall's college library), there is a Norman crypt. In that crypt is supposed to be an entrance to a network of tunnels extending under the city, that were used up until the 1960s (although no mention is made on several sites describing the crypt). A church has existed on the current site since the late 10th century. In the 11th century, it was replaced by a stone church, which is mentioned in Domesday Book of 1085: The Norman parts of the current church were built around 1140 by Robert D'Oyley, who was then Governor of Oxford. The church passed to the Crown from D'Oyley's heirs. Again, this is the same connection as Wallingford.

There are also extensive tunnels that are known about and to some level still used under the area of the Bodleian Library. Whilst the Bodleian Library, in its current incarnation, has a continuous history dating back to 1602, its roots date back even further to the University Church of St. Mary the Virgin on the High Street. A church was established on this site, at the centre of the old walled city, in Anglo-Saxon times; records of 1086 note the church as previously belonging to an estate held by Aubrey de Coucy. In the early days of Oxford University, the church was adopted as the first building of the university, congregation met there from at least 1252, and by the early 13th century it was the seat of university government. Around 1320, a two-storey building was added to the north side of the chancel – the upper storey housed books bequeathed by Thomas Cobham, Bishop of Worcester, which formed the first university library.

What makes much of this interesting is the geographical locations of some of the buildings and the references, like those in Wallingford, to "closed up doorways leading to a network of tunnels." The proximity of some key buildings is shown below[50].

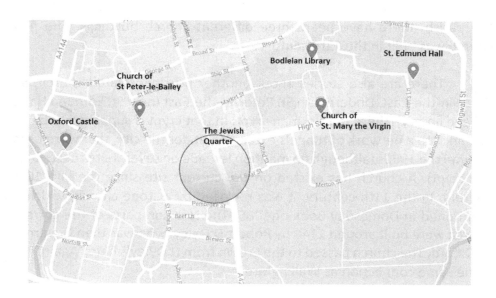

The furthest distance – between St. Edmund Hall, which was the original St. Peter-in-the-East, to a supposed entrance to a network of tunnels – is just 1,000 metres from the castle. St. Peter-le-Bailey – the original closest church – was just over 120 metres, certainly close enough to be connected. Finally, there are stories about tunnels between all the houses in the Jewish Quarter. The Normans had encouraged Jews to settle to help build trade and commerce.

The medieval Jewish Quarter was situated in today's St. Aldate's, then called the Great Jewry. Beneath the houses of the Quarter (where Santander bank, Oxford Town Hall and the Citizens' Advice Bureau are now located), a network of tunnels connected the vaulted basements of all the Jewish houses. Like all of the basement doorways in the street, they were bricked up in the 1930s. As non-Christians, Jews were not "subjects of the realm" but were wards of the Crown and therefore under royal protection.

The King could turn to the Jews as his own private source of income and would tax them heavily for certain projects such as funding wars.

So, oxford holds some interesting parallels to Wallingford in terms of location, type of building, use of the building, surrounding churches and relationship with the community. However, once again, while there are solid facts about crypts and cellars under specific locations, as well as limited tunnels, such as in the Jewish Quarter, there is almost no factual evidence of a network of tunnels on a larger scale. Even the tunnel under the Bodleian dates to a later period and appears to again have been built on a "building to building" basis, and not part of a network.

Northampton Castle

Let "friends of Northampton Castle" do our introduction. *"Soon after the Romans left Britain in 410, Northampton was establishing itself as a local seat of power with Saxon defenses near the site of the Castle and St Peter's church. There were Saxon buildings in the area around Sol Central and St. Peter's church, and by the early 11th century, Northampton had connections to powerful people of the time."* So again, an interesting historical background to the site and linkages to church buildings in the area.

Not much of the castle remains and apparently there are few drawings or depictions of the site itself. A survey of the castle in 1322–3 indicates that the castle contained a great hall with a long chamber adjacent to the hall to the east, and the great chamber next to the hall to the west. There was also a lower chapel. Besides a new tower there were six small towers. A keep is mentioned and a further chapel; one of the chapels was dedicated to St. George.

There is also a parish Church of All Saints that contains a crypt, but this appears to date to the 14th century; there appear to be no indication of tunnels out of the crypt. However once again there are stories[51]: *"According to local historian and founder trustee of the Holy Sepulchre*

95

Restoration Trust John Kightley MBE, many of these cellars (under the city) are thought to have originated from church buildings centered around the market square, and All Saints Church. Fifteen years ago, John was told by a colleague at The Holy Sepulchre Church about a large tunnel under the building. 'It has been said by historians that medieval tunnels ran from the church to Delapre Abbey, and this could be one of them.' John was fascinated and brought in his son Peter who was studying Geophysics at Birmingham University to find out more about the tunnels underneath the church. Using electronic ground radar equipment to measure the earth's movement Peter found something quite intriguing. John was ecstatic, 'The equipment went crazy, there was a lot of movement under the church which suggested there may be more cellars but as we haven't been able to gain access underneath it, we cannot physically prove anything'." Once again, the stories are there and some clues, but limited access stops further investigation. We have yet another story from the same BBC source, however.

"Before the Northampton Train Station was built in 1859 the site was occupied by Northampton Castle. The castle was the site of Parliament for over 200 years and used regularly by the Royal family. It was said that this castle had a tunnel linking it to All Saints Church. This tunnel, some historians claim, may have been used by Thomas Becket to escape from the castle and the town on his way to France."

The final word goes to Wikipedia[52] *"It is said by some that, underneath the streets of the town of Northampton in England, there remains a labyrinth of tunnels, along with many cellars and ancient crypts from the past. Much of the present town's development took place during medieval times. There are certainly a number of cellars, some of them medieval. Some of them are connected and some may have been connected in the past. It is doubtful if they ever have formed an extensive connected network. Many of these cellars are thought to have originated from the church buildings, that today are centred on All Saints Church – for instance underneath the Northampton & County Club in George Row (opposite the church) some fine vaulted cellars can be seen. There are similar tunnels on the other side of the church at Drum Lane – underneath what was the Shipman's public house. John Speed's map of Northampton from 1610 shows that the church was then the largest landowner in the town. Clashes took place over the years between the church and the monarchy – such as the banning of markets being held in the churchyards. It is thought that some of these tunnels were established as escape routes for clergy during times of trouble. The various religious houses in early times were found at all the main 8 compass points – giving rise to a series of radial tunnels heading out from All Saints Church at the centre of town to the various houses."*

Once again, we have a great deal of history – in fact, Northampton Castle location and the city itself would date back at least as far as Wallingford and archeology seems similar in the finds that have been made. The castle, its history, the relationship to local churches, possible escape routes out of the castle, all contribute to the possibility of a "network of tunnels." But sadly, once again there is limited evidence.

Other castles, some Norman

In this section we look at similar castles to those identified above except that these appear not to have been "built or sanctioned" directly by William's initial construction programme, or they were from a later date but might be relevant. However, they all hold some stories.

Farleigh and Hungerford Castle

This location has been included because "Visit Britain[53]" suggest it as a location of "Castle dungeons." However, it was not a Norman Castle. Farleigh and Hungerford Castle was begun before 1383 by Sir Thomas Hungerford (c. 1328–1397). Thomas prospered as chief land steward of Edward III's fourth son, John of Gaunt, Duke of Lancaster. The castle was built on the site of an earlier, possibly 13th century manor house, which Sir Thomas had bought in 1369. Essentially a symbol of his rising status, Sir Thomas's building (which later became the inner court of the extended castle) was a fortified mansion ranged around a rectangular central courtyard, with a tall tower at each corner, in the 'quadrangular' style fashionable during the 1370s and 1380s. There is also a chapel, St. Leonard's, which stands in the outer court of Farleigh; there is a crypt located under the chapel. There were also dungeons including an "oubliette."

There are however no further stories of tunnels or indications of connections between "The Castle" and outside. It appears to have been built as a residence rather than a fortification, especially since the location was overlooked by higher ground.

Pontefract Castle

The attraction of Pontefract Castle comes from the great write up on the Exploring Castles website[54] that includes the following: *"The most terrifying castle dungeons in the whole of England were undoubtedly those of Pontefract Castle, in Yorkshire. Pontefract Castle was a vast and fearsome fortress with a blood-curdling reputation – it was so notorious that it was depicted in Shakespeare's play, Richard III. In the play, Earl Rivers describes Pontefract (then Pomfret) as: "O Pomfret, Pomfret! O thou bloody prison! Fatal and ominous to noble peers". Pontefract Castle was used as a prison in the 1300s, and King Richard II of England was almost certainly murdered in cold-blood in the castle dungeons. The dungeons where huge, and extended across a number of different rooms, all around 35ft below the main bulk of the castle."*

It appears that the entire place was constructed on an old Anglo-Saxon burial ground. The castle was constructed on a rock to the east of the town above All Saints' Church. It appears that little survives other than parts of the curtain wall and excavated and tidied inner walls. It had inner and outer baileys. Parts of a 12th century wall and the Piper Tower's postern gate and the foundations of a chapel are the oldest remains; the Chapel was St. Clement's. The ruins of the Round Tower or keep are on the original 11th century mound. The Great Gate is flanked by 14th century semi-circular towers and had inner and outer barbicans. Chambers excavated into the rock in the inner bailey possibly indicate the site of the old hall and the North Bailey gate is marked by the remains of a rectangular tower.

Pontefract has a huge and (according to Exploring Castles[55]) oppressive network of dungeons – hollowed out of the bedrock 35 feet below the castle. Prisoners were trapped in the winding, pitch-black pits for weeks at a time, and scratched their names into the walls during their miserable imprisonment. We are told *"You can see the prisoner's names, scratched into the dungeon walls, when you visit the castle today, as part of the tour to the 'magazines and armour cellars"* – these cellars were originally the dungeons.

There are also tunnels and cellars below what is believed to have been the great hall that were later used as ammunition storage (named the "magazine"). There are also stories on a Facebook website including links to pictures of tunnels that suggest tunnels do exist here. There is also some ongoing discussion about people who have apparently either seen these tunnels or had firsthand stories.

This was from a Facebook post related to Featherstone[56], which is near Pontefract. *"It is said that whilst the new road was being dug into the limestone that the contractors found a hole. The hole was opened and found to be a tunnel. The tunnel was the one from All Saints church to Pontefract castle. The tunnel was stone lined and did contain methane. The side walls of the road as you see them now, cover the entrance on either side. The road has now blocked the link from Featherstone to Pontefract. It is said that from the church the tunnel ran to Pontefract. What is not known is where else it goes. It was suggested that the tunnel could go to the monastery at Nostel. It was also said that the tunnel had an entrance via a grave in the church yard."*

Included in these accounts was another intriguing story which also has links to pictures. *"The first ever pictures of one of these tunnels; no one has been down there in over 400 years. The tunnel varies in height and pans out about 3 ft. It is carved out of the rock, and you can see the chisel marks and a ledge carved on the right side. I think I was about 10ft down. the tunnel comes to an end. by the look at the chisel marks, I bet it goes down but is full off dirt. It was suggested that the tunnel could go to the monastery at Nostel. It was also said that the tunnel had an entrance via a grave in the church yard."*

The left hand picture appears[57] to be the "magazine" under the great hall and the other passage is not identified but could reflect on of the others that were found.

Pontefract was also the site of Pontefract Priory, a Cluniac priory founded in 1090 by Robert de Lacy dedicated to St. John the Evangelist. The priory was dissolved by royal authority in 1539. So, we have again the connections with a castle, internal chapel, crypts, other churches – and stories about external tunnels. It appears that some of the stories might be supported by facts, but the postings are over 10 years old and difficult to follow up.

Carmarthen Castle

'Henry I' established his own domain within South Wales in the early 12th century, in order to assert his authority. He took this action after a number of individuals had exercised their right to take territory in Wales independently and so were outside royal supervision. He chose Carmarthen, a site that had previously been a Roman fort and walled town, which was centrally located between Pembroke and Gower. Carmarthen Castle already existed by the time Henry I decided to take control of the area. It had been built no later than 1094 by William fitzBaldwin on top of a steep buff overlooking the bridging point over the River Tywi. The castle took the form of an earth and timber motte-and-bailey fortification. The motte was topped with a timber palisade and round tower. There were two baileys – the rectangular Inner Ward housed the main domestic and administrative functions, whilst the smaller Outer Ward may have been used for livestock.

The website for Wales Online[58] lays out some of the key stories related to tunnels. *"One historical point of interest that still finds its home between fact and legend is the 'Tunnels of Carmarthen' – a sprawling network of ancient passageways that, according to rumour, connect different important points of the ancient town."*

One man who insists he has trodden the ground underneath the streets is retired building control officer, Geraint Jones. He once braved the myth and walked from the Old Market Square Delicatessen, at the corner of Nott Square, all the way down as far as the Guildhall, without touching the pavement. *"There was a doorway and behind it was an alleyway; I walked underneath the pavement all the way down to where Woolworths used to be. I didn't go any further because it was pitch black!"* Asked later by Robert Harries of Wales Online, Lisa Rees, the owner of the delicatessen, said*: "Yes, there is a cellar here with a doorway that leads off into something else."* Harries went through the door, to the right, slowly along this tunnel; about 20ft along, the exploration comes to an end. To the right, a blocked-up wall, no way through. To the left, another room, but more bricks and no access further down.

They go on to tell the story of Darryn Davies, who runs Floral Decor in King Street along with his partner, Sienna, who says *"lots of people have been into the store to enquire about the tunnels. We've had about 15 people coming in all asking the same thing – can we have a look at your cellar? They've all been absolutely fascinated by the idea that there's a tunnel that runs underneath the shop, or at least used to. The floor to the cellar is uneven, and people have said that's down to an old Roman Road being underneath. There is a section of the cellar, which is formed like a tunnel, but there's no access to it at either end, only through a side door. Some people have mentioned that the tunnel may have gone from the castle all the way to the church, but I don't know about that."*

The stories go on to ask, *"Is it true that these underground tunnels once provided high-profile prisoners with a safe route from Carmarthen Castle to St Peter's Church, allowing them to transport themselves in peace between captivity and the sanctuary of their place of worship?"* It is not known whether an older, pre-Norman church originally stood on the site, but St. Peter's lies within the site of Roman Moridinum, inside the presumed west gate of the Roman walls. The church, if founded soon after the construction of the Norman castle, was located midway between the castle and the monastic settlement of Llandeulyddog, which is known to have existed before the Norman Conquest. Its location would have allowed it to serve the spiritual needs of both the Welsh community of Old Carmarthen, and New Carmarthen which developed in the shadow of the castle.

Wales Online continues the story: *"One man who may know is the current vicar of St Peter's Church, Canon Leigh Richardson. Walking through the church, he recalls an incident which suggested an ancient route to the castle could well have existed. 'We had a plumbing problem here a few years ago,' he says. 'A plumber came out and lifted up one of the heating grids that we have on the floor to get underneath. There's a drop of about six feet and there are pipes that travel from one end of the church to the other. When he was down there, he said that he could feel that underneath the ground was hollow, as if there was something else lower down.' It wouldn't be unusual for a church to have a route to the castle in years gone by, mainly for safety. There may have been situations when people might have wanted to travel between the two without wanting to attract public attention. In those days, the castle and the church were the two main symbols of power."*

Not content to focus on recent stories, an article in the August 24th, 1906, edition of the *Carmarthen Journal*, quoted the following: *"The entrance is now covered over by tiled flooring but P.S. Davies of the Carmarthen Borough Police states on one occasion that he attempted to descend the passage and found a flight of steps leading down. He, however, failed to penetrate any appreciable distance owing to the very foul condition of the air there, but he went far enough to see a passage big enough for a man to walk along it, and running parallel with Priory Street in the direction of Ivy Bush."*

There is an access to the dungeons beneath the castle that can still be seen but actual exploration of any further tunnels or passages has not been reported. So again, we have the castle, possible Roman ruins, churches, a potential priory, and dungeons plus lots of stories and some closed up doorways. There's great potential for tunnels but not much else.

Knaresborough Castle

It appears that Knaresborough Castle goes back to at least 1100 AD when a Norman baron erected a simple fortification on a high cliff above the River Nidd, looking over Knaresborough Forest. There may have been a fortification here earlier. The town's name was recorded as 'Chednaresburg' in Domesday Book of 1086. The suffix 'burg' comes from the Saxon word 'burh', meaning a fortified settlement. That fortification was probably little more than an earthwork ditch and bank, perhaps topped with a timber palisade, but could it have been similar to the burh at Wallingford?

In 1648, on instructions from Parliament, the castle was to be thoroughly demolished. Most of the curtain wall and buildings were destroyed. However, the townspeople petitioned Parliament and complete demolition was halted, so that some aspects of the castle remain. These include the courthouse that had been established since Tudor times and the keep that was often used to hold prisoners. Similar to Wallingford, all usable stone, lead and timber from the roofs and windows were sold off to raise money for the Treasury. Many town centre buildings were built of 'castle stone'.

Here, there is some evidence of tunnels remaining as part of the ruins[59]. Sometime in the late 13th century or early 14th century two sally ports were built, reached by secret underground tunnels.

These sally ports might be used to launch an unexpected attack on a besieging army, or simply to sneak in and out of the castle without being seen. The tunnels leading to the sally ports were large enough for a small band of armed men to pass through. The tunnels were cut into the solid rock and roofed with rubble mortar. They slope steeply down to the level of the bottom of the dry moat to a hidden exit.

One of these remains open to the public and provides some idea of the construction of the tunnels from this period. The picture above reflects the exhibit that is open to the public.

Once again, there is potential for tunnels but little to demonstrate a significant network or access external to the castle.

Carlisle Castle

Carlisle is included as, once again, Visit Britain identifies it as a location with "historic dungeons." Carlisle Castle was built during the reign of William II of England, the son of William the Conqueror. At that time, Cumberland (the original name for north and west Cumbria) was still considered a part of Scotland. William II ordered the construction of a Norman style motte-and-bailey castle in Carlisle on the site of the old Roman fort of Luguvalium, (dated to 72 AD), with the castle construction beginning in 1093. The need for a castle in Carlisle was to keep the northern border of England secured against the threat of invasion from Scotland. In 1122, Henry I of England ordered a stone castle to be constructed on the site. In 1644 Carlisle Castle suffered an 8-month siege.

The most important battles for the city of Carlisle and its castle were during the Jacobite rising of 1745 against George II. That battle marked the end of the castle's fighting life, as defending the border between England and Scotland was not necessary with both countries united in Great Britain. After 1746, the castle became somewhat neglected, although some minor repairs were undertaken such as that of the drawbridge in 1783. Some parts of the castle were then demolished for use as raw materials in the 19th century to create more or less what is visible to the visitor today.

Carlisle Castle boasts an impressive record of royal plots and prisoners, including Mary, Queen of Scots. However, it is the dungeons below that saw a more common breed of prisoner, and in which lies a brutal reminder of a sinister story the castle has to tell. Prisoners held during the Jacobite War were kept in such appalling conditions that they were reduced to licking the walls of the dungeon for moisture. Coined the 'licking stones,' these haunting relics can be seen in the castle today. There were stories of a tunnel that linked Carlisle Castle with the Cathedral. It was said that Mary Queen of Scots used the tunnel as an escape route.

It seems that the dungeons are indeed the main feature of passages or tunnels for Carlisle Castle. Little else seems to suggest that there were other access routes.

Framlingham Castle

While Framlingham does not appear to be an early Norman Castle, it could still hold some relevant stories. The first documentary reference to a castle at Framlingham occurs in 1148; however, the actual date of its construction is uncertain. It may have been built by Roger Bigod in either the late 11th century or around 1100. A second possibility is that Roger's son, Hugh Bigod, built it during the years of the Anarchy in the 1140s on the site of an existing manor house; and a third possibility is that there were in fact two castles: the first being built in the late 11th century and then demolished by Hugh Bigod in the 1160s to make way for a newer, larger castle. Historian Magnus Alexander hypothesizes that the castle might have been built on top of a set of pre-existing Anglo Saxon, high prestige buildings.

The website Hidden East Anglia[60] provides a number of stories about tunnels and passages. This one related to Framlingham tells us: *"Leiston Abbey was founded in 1182 but moved slightly inland in 1363. Two tunnels are said to begin at the west end of the neat abbey ruins, the first running for about 4½ miles to Greyfriars at Dunwich where there are scant remains of a 13th century Franciscan friary on the cliff edge). A. J. Forrest claimed in 1961 to have been shown, in a corner of the refectory at Leiston, the entrance to a passage said to run all the way to Framlingham. Other sources state definitely that the destination was the 12th century Framlingham Castle (pre 1148).*

"Forrest records that along this tunnel 'a sow and her litter' once wandered and were never seen again. As usual, a blocked drainage channel has been held responsible for the legends. Part way (and roughly on a straight line) between Leiston and Framlingham is Saxmundham, where a tunnel was reported leading from the 16th century former Angel Inn to

Leiston Abbey and extending in the opposite direction towards Framlingham. The 'East Anglian Daily Times' of November 13th, 1987, noted that a 'Mr. P' had found the tunnels to run 26 feet underground and were big enough to allow the passage of a horse and cart. Supposedly, a "large, brick-lined tunnel" was found on this general alignment in the early 1970's when a parking lot was being constructed in Saxmundham."

So, we again have stories of the same "types" of tunnels that many of the other accounts, but no pictures or archeological facts or existing ruins to support it or look at.

Stories about other tunnels under towns

There are many, many other stories about passageways and tunnels in older towns and cities across the UK. A few of these are shown here to broaden the research of impossibility, possibility, probability, and certainty that might add to or support the Wallingford stories. Given that we discussed East Anglia[61] already, we can add a few more from there. The references can be accessed to look at more detail.

Lavenham: Some 15th century houses in Water Street have long been known as the 'Priory', but evidence for an actual religious foundation is lacking. In the cellars is supposed to be a blocked entrance into an underground watercourse, and opposite, another door to a tunnel which leads towards Lady Street. Cellars beneath are said to be 14th century, and to have another blocked entranceway to a passage that runs along under the road. One passage is rumoured to lead to the 'Priory' itself. At the same time as a 'Roman bath or crypt' was supposedly found here, traces of a tunnel were found leading from a building in the gardens towards the 16th century Guildhall in the marketplace.

Lawshall: Lawshall Hall has the date 1557 over a door, some features said to be 'ecclesiastical-looking' and is supposed to have been once a monastery; this probably came about simply because the manor was once the property of the Benedictine abbey of Ramsey in

Huntingdonshire. A tunnel is said to run from here to the 16th century Coldham Hall in Stanningfield, a mile north. This mansion was built in 1574 by Robert Rookwood, whose son Ambrose was a co-conspirator with Guy Fawkes. The Rookwood's were diehard Catholics when such were classed as heretics, so it's hardly surprising that the Hall is riddled with passages and bolt-holes. One hiding-place can be entered from the steps of the north wing staircase, and another from the fireplace in the dining room.

Lowestoft: For about 200 years there has been a tradition that much of the northern end of the old town is built over the remains of a monastery, but there's no recorded evidence for it. The existence of crypt-like cellars with groined roofs and arches under some of the buildings in the High Street is often taken as proof, but in fact they are simply merchant's cellars of the 14/15th centuries. The accidental discovery of parts of these in the early 1900s led to much speculation about a network of tunnels connecting one side of the High Street with the other, and with the 15th century church of St. Margaret half a mile to the west. The houses on the east side have their backs to the sea cliff, so it's perhaps inevitable that smugglers would be credited with using the tunnels – although monks, or even Oliver Cromwell, are given the honour of having constructed them. A tunnel is also said to run from the High Street to Oulton High House, almost two miles away. This Elizabethan manor house stood empty for some time in the late 1700s, during which time it was used by local smugglers as a temporary store for their contraband. A local man said that he had lifted a flag stone in the floor and gone down the tunnel when a lad – but this was probably just an access into the 14th century crypt beneath the high altar.

Then there is talk about tunnels in Teesside[62]; this story is about what is below a pub called The Monk that was being renovated: *"Legend has it that a network of underground tunnels leads to and from the town's historic priory. Over the years, there's been talk of tunnels haunted by a "Black Monk" and ones which 12th century monks would walk through to visit ladies of ill repute, passing on their way a chest of gold coins guarded by a raven. Steve Hewison, who has opened the bar with Peter and Alan*

Milburn, said: 'It's probably either a priest's hole, where priests used to hide when Catholics were persecuted, a cellar, or it was part of a tunnel network that goes across to the priory. There certainly seems to be part of the wall which has been blocked up, so maybe that led to the tunnel'."

Swindon[63] is another unlikely candidate for old underground passages. *"In a recent find under Villetts House in Cricklade Street, a door of 10-inch-thick steel in the basement was opened to reveal a network of three bricked up tunnels as wide as a double decker bus. It is believed that this is just a small section of a series of tunnels running under Old Town – a network that could extend as far as the Lawns and even out to Coate Water over a mile away. Years ago, I heard that there is/was a tunnel from St Mary`s church to the Cheney Manor House. It was said to be intended as an escape route for monks trapped in the church by the Normans ! I believe that 'recent' efforts to locate it have failed!"*

An interested reader could do a lot more research; there is information going back both hundreds and thousands of years, for more stories. The challenge seems to be that there are many stories but little proof. Sure, there are tunnels and passages but the evidence anywhere of an extensive network seems to be hard to come by. In the final chapter we can compare what has been found with the limited research, with the stories from Wallingford. Then the reader can decide – are the tunnels fact or fiction?

Fact or Fiction?

At this point there are stories about Wallingford as well as examples of similar towns, including those that have similar castles. We have limited proof about tunnels under Wallingford, but it seems that is the situation elsewhere: lots of stories but limited proof of the existence of tunnels – especially the idea of an extensive network. Is Wallingford unique enough that, while the stories have not (yet) been proven elsewhere, they could actually be true for Wallingford?

Given how long ago some of the hidden tunnels might have been created, it is not surprising that little can be found; this would be especially true of those that date back to, or even before Roman times – even though we know that the Romans were accomplished engineers for roads, buildings, tunnels, aqueducts, and many other structures. We know that while much of this was developed "at home," as their empire expanded so did their application of engineering skills.

Even so, many of the tunnels that may have been constructed after the Roman era have probably disappeared as time passed and populations increased. The combination of geographic expansion of residential and commercial areas and the demolition and new construction that have taken place over at least 1,500 years has obliterated much of historical evidence. Until recently, these cycles took place with zero or limited archeological oversight, meaning that history is, in many cases, buried deep down. While modern geophysical as well as computing capabilities and, more recently, artificial intelligence, are gradually increasing abilities to see deeper and deeper with excavation, there remains the problem that many of the possible locations have been built over, in many cases several times, and are therefore inaccessible.

As the population has grown, there has been a need for dwellings and supporting infrastructure. As wealth developed and economic eras advanced, more and more areas that might have been undisturbed have been covered up. In 1066, the population of England was estimated to be between 2.0 and 2.5 million, yet this was a significant reduction from the Roman period, when it is estimated to have been about 4 million. The following chart shows some key statistics. One of the issues to remember is that during these periods the country suffered plagues that killed substantial numbers; many people immigrated and emigrated; life expectancy significantly increased and infant mortality significantly decreased. Additionally, economic, and social aspects of life changed significantly, especially with Britain's leading role in the industrial revolution. These facts not only reflected overall growth and increased density, but it also created "churn" as buildings were pulled down and rebuilt. Population of England (numbers are approximate):

Year	Population	Density
300	3.0 million	23 / sq. km.
1086	1.7 million	13 / sq. km.
1200	3.4 million	26 / sq. km.
1400	2.1 million	16 / sq. km.
1600	4.1 million	31 / sq. km.
1800	5.2 million	39 / sq. km.
2000	49.1 million	376 / sq. km.

It can be seen that between 1800 and 2000 the population growth spiralled, and it was mostly in this period that a great deal of the history would have been built over. (Also note the density which would have significant impact because of the expansion and re-building in the cities where older properties such as Castles were situated.)

So, what do we know after all this? While it is up to the reader to decide, here are a few thoughts and conclusions that I have arrived at, starting with how we might "classify" the ideas:

1. Nothing is impossible because we do not have all the facts.
2. some things are unlikely or improbable based on what we have learned and basic logical thought.
3. some things are possible based on what we have learned; and
4. there are certain ideas that are probable.

I have to repeat that I am entirely unqualified in any way to assess historical, archeological, or other facts, hypotheses and conclusions researched and / or arrived at by others. These are just my opinions. I will start in reverse order.

Probable ideas

From the research it appears that castles typically had dungeons that were below ground and sometimes accessed by passages. Some may have been long or short depending upon each situation. This would support some of the early stories about tunnels leading to dungeons under Wallingford Castle.

It also seems likely that there were one or more short access tunnels allowing access to or escape from a castle, which opened outside via a postern door of some sort. In the case of Wallingford, this might explain the tunnel found "heading east towards the river" and this particular could also be for purposes of access for arrivals and departures from the river. The idea of a short escape tunnel might explain the boathouse "renovation" story (from the Nautical Wheel) and, if the outer earthworks are eventually confirmed in the Thames Street, it could explain one or more stories there.

It also appears that many churches built before, during and after the periods we have researched, including those within or close by castles, had underground crypts that were once again accessed by tunnels and passages. It seems that St. Mary Le More, as well as St. Peter's had crypts of some type, and it is probable that the older churches, most of which have now disappeared, also had these.

It also appears that, in many situations, and Wallingford in particular, there might have been passages beneath ground between the church and the house (next door) where the minister lived. This could explain several of the Wallingford "bricked up doorways." As examples, this might be the case for St. Mary Le More and the tunnel by Church Lane in what used to be St. Mary's Church House. It might also explain a link between St. Peter-in-the-West and Stone Hall, and St. Mary the Less and doorways under properties in St. Mary's Street or High Street. These hidden access routes would be for both convenience and safety. This might also contribute to the Thames Street tunnel story, relative to the old St. Michael's church.

So overall there probably are passageways, tunnels, and bricked-up doorways that date from medieval times and were for "limited access purposes."

Possible ideas

It is possible that some of the connections between churches, other religious buildings and elsewhere could have extended further. As an example, the tunnel under Flint House could have been an access tunnel to other parts of the (original) church of St. Nicholas and to the Priory.

It is also possible that there was a number of connections between individual properties in the area around the Lamb Hotel, and particularly the north side of High Street. This was apparently the "Jewish Quarter" of Wallingford and, according to the history of Oxford, there were doorways and connecting tunnels between all of the Jewish residences.

The tunnels at the east end of High Street on the north side might possibly have been access points to the Castle to avoid passing through the Castle gates – maybe even part of the escape / access tunnels.

It is also a possibility that there may have been one or more tunnels connecting All Saints' Church with the inside of the Castle, if this church was "the Church of Royalty at Wallingford Castle" before St. Nicholas was completed inside the fortifications, so there may well have been hidden access points to allow people to move without being seen and in safety.

There also may well have been access tunnels between properties on High Street, in particular from the area around the George Hotel, which had belonged to high-ranking officials, and the Castle for access purposes. These may have even existed prior to the Norman building phase. There may also have been a connection between the old St. Martin's Church and All Saints' Church, which would run under High Street under what is now the Lamb and back parallel to Castle Street. More research into the founding, funding, patronage, and priests of all the Wallingford churches would have to be carried out to add any credence to this possibility.

It is also possible that there was a main passageway running along the eastern end of High Street that several properties had access to, which was created as a hidden access for people in those properties at the time. These may have been military personnel and others having relationships including business with the Castle – again before or after the Norman period.

It is also possible that there may have been a connection between St. Mary Le More and St. Mary Church House that then went along the west side of the Market Place and joined up with St. Martin's. This might explain the doorway found during the renovations to KP Stationers in the Market Place.

What concerns me about many of these stories about access between the Town and the interior of the Castle is the nature of the sieges that took place. If there had been access tunnels would the last siege by Stephen have ended the way that it did? Surely provisions would have been able to be delivered into the Castle.

The siege stories raise some other possibilities. Given the resources that Stephen put into making his siege successful and his construction of a fort opposite the Castle on the Crowmarsh side of the river, it might be possible that there was indeed a complete or partial tunnel under the Thames which was created as they tried to "dig their way in." It is also possible that this might contribute to stories about tunnels as the St. Peter's end of High Street, adjacent to Calleva House, assuming Stephen did create a base on the west side of the Thames.

Finally, it does seem possible that, given the involvement between the Crown, nobility and the Church and the timing of the building of Wallingford Castle and the Priory, there could have been hidden tunnels between the Castle and the Priory. There seem to be two choices of connections – either from the Priory via the Bull Croft under the baileys to the inner part of the Castle, maybe even connecting to the chapel, or church and / or college? (Also connecting with All Hallows / All Saints)? And the alternative would be a passageway heading parallel to or under High Street to join up with possible tunnels at the Lamb crossroads.

Improbable

I am sure there will those who look upon the last section and say that some or all of my suggestions should be in this section as "improbable." Maybe – but again, that is the reader's choice. It does seem to me that certain stories of tunnels are indeed improbable.

First of these would be the various stories about tunnels to "distant places" such as Ewelme or Dorchester. I believe that these pertain to above-ground routes that connected the Castle and these locations, but which may have been accessed through tunnels under the bailey and moats of the Castle. It also would appear that tunnels that extend a long way from the High Street area to a few select points would also be improbable. As an example, the Corn Exchange is more likely a "one-off" cellar or storage area. Also, the Thames Street location is more likely a "stand-alone" story. Note, I do not say impossible, for lengthy tunnels did exist; Ewelme, for example, was known to have become a favourite place for Henry compared to the "cold and drafty" Wallingford Castle in its later years and it is possible that they could have had a tunnel dug – but not likely.

Crowmarsh Hill is another interesting possibility even if improbable; if the siege forts built by Stephen in Crowmarsh did exist and if there were any sort of tunnels or ground works in that area, then the probability of extending these tunnels to a "look out" or escape point on Crowmarsh Hill might be possible – or even the extension to French Gardens at Howbery Park.

Possibility or probability

Using the discussions above we can look at the stories told about Wallingford that were detailed earlier and see what this might look like.

The solid lines on the map[64] represent probability, the larger dashed lines possibilities and the small, dashed line possibility – but at the low end of the scale.

1. The link between St. Peter in the West and Stone Hall
2. Flint House to "parts of" the Priory
3. Link between St. Martin's and All Hallows / All Saints
4. Link between All Hallows / All Saints and the Castle
5. Possible tunnels in the Jewish Quarter
6. Possible "nobility link" between High Street (probably around The George) and inside the Castle.
7. Possible tunnels around dungeons (especially "Cloere Brien") and elsewhere in the Castle (could also link to an outside exit)
8. The known (?) tunnel "running east toward the river"

9.   Possible tunnel from High Street to inside first gates
10. Highly speculative (but possible) tunnel connecting the Priory with
     Al Saints / All Hallows and from there to inside the Castle.

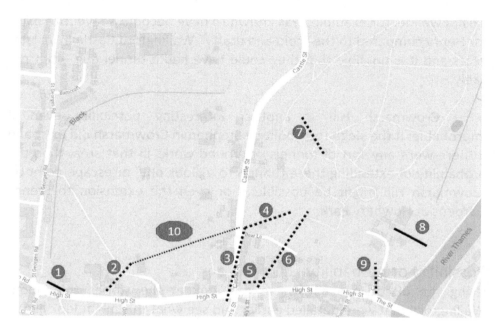

One can see that all this might be pure speculation but based on a review of the stories and facts, if one were to look for potential tunnels, these might be the general locations (and once again "deep down").

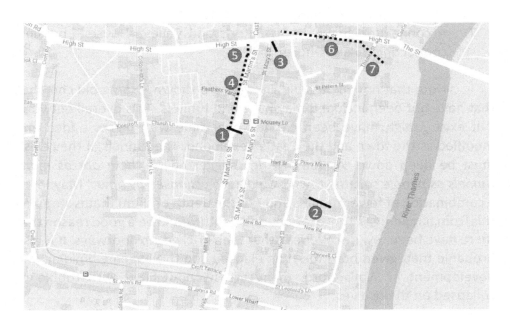

The other (south) side of High Street might look a bit more "sparse." This reflects the idea that in all probability tunnels would have been in a more concentrated area. However, once again, given the importance of the Market Place over the centuries, it is not impossible that there could be other locations – just with few, if any, stories.

1. The tunnel between St. Mary Le More and the Church house (minister's residence maybe?).
2. The possible tunnel between St. Martin's and either the minister's house and / or another location in the Thames Street area.
3. The tunnel between St. Mary the Less and a minister's house somewhere in the St. Mary's Street / High Street area.
4. A possible tunnel connecting the church house of St. Mary Le More and St. Martins.
5. Possible St. Martin's Church connection to minister's house (and possibly back to St. Mary Le More).
6. The "tunnels of High Street" suggesting a passage the length of the street that various properties had access to that eventually

connected with a tunnel to the Castle.

7. A connection between St. Peter's and Calleva House – possibly connecting up elsewhere.

Note that not all possible linkages are shown – some old churches that have not been included may have had tunnels. This overall network, if it exists, might have been created over time with pieces added and modified as the town and the Castle developed. The tunnels, if they exist, must be deep down. As Judy Dewey suggested *"if there are as many tunnels as people say, the town would have collapsed by now."* Maybe it's a combination of fewer tunnels and / or the depth of them that is stopping this from happening? The locations and depth would be a good reason that there have been few discoveries other than bricked-up doorways. It is also probable that, given both the time elapsed and the ongoing building and development in Wallingford, many are by now filled with rubble or collapsed on themselves.

Who knows? Maybe one day some or all of the possible tunnels may give up their secrets. Maybe technology will come to the aid of explorers and help identify possible remains that still exist? Who knows what construction event or accident may suddenly open up access to an otherwise unknown space? It is all speculation! For now, the question must remain, "Are Wallingford tunnels fact or fiction?"

About the author and the Shepherd family

Nick Shepherd was born in Didcot in 1946; his mother and her family were from Didcot and his father, Arthur Shepherd, and his family, were from Wallingford. The Shepherds had come to Wallingford in the early 1900's where his grandfather established a grocery business, initially as Crane & Shepherd, and after the early 1930's as Leonard Shepherd Limited.

Arthur's brother Alec as the eldest was supposed to take over the family business but was killed in Sicily landings. Before the war, Arthur had trained in London as a professional hairdresser and the family has already established a men's hair salon on High Street. However, on his return from the war, where he had spent five years in prisoner of war camp after being captured at Dunkirk (he was a medic and stayed behind with the injured), it fell to him to take over the family grocery business.

These were good times as the country recovered after the war and the business grew and expanded. The original retail grocery business at 77 High Street was expanded several times and as the new wholesale business grew, that eventually had to be re-located. The hair-dressing business had also expanded to include both male and female salons. By this time Flint House, the family home was empty following the death of Arthur's parents and so this became the location of the wholesale business.

In the late 1950's competition from the "new" supermarkets started to impact many of the local retail businesses. Sadly, the combination of this, and the lingering effects of what is now known as PTSD, five years as a POW, and a failed marriage, took its' toll on Arthur who, after several efforts at rehabilitation, died in 1966. By this time, the creditors had moved in and all the businesses as well as the family home had been sold off.

As was typical in smaller towns and communities the local businesses and their owners, were heavily involved in the community. The Arthur Shepherd Trophy is still awarded annually by the Wallingford Allotments and Garden Society (for Specialties - Open). Leonard Shepherd was one of the initial members of the Comrades Club and for many years his billiard cue had a place of honour in the snooker / billiard hall. He was also an early supporter of the Wallingford Rowing Club and both he and Arthur were active members of the St. Hilda Lodge of the Masons. (Arthur and his wife were organizers for many years of the annual "Ladies Night" for the Lodge). Leonard Shepherd was Mayor of Wallingford in 1931 and 1932.

Arthur was active in establishing the Wallingford Swimming Pool and the Portcullis Tennis Club and was also a Special Constable; he was also active in the Chamber of Trade. His wife was an early member of Sinodun Players, from a time when the meetings were held at Mrs. Curtis house in Sotwell; and she taught dancing for the Sinodun players for several years in the late 1950's and early 1960's and was also an active member of the tennis club.

After Arthur's death, Nick continued the Wallingford legacy and tradition by marrying Janet, the daughter of another established Wallingford family. Janet was one of two daughters of Maurice Johnstone - one of four boys of the Johnstone family that had owned Reynolds & Johnstone, which had previously been Upton and Reynolds, with both Upton and then Reynolds leaving the business. This family was again an active part of the community, including Janet's uncle James (J.O.) Johnstone who served as mayor of Wallingford at the time of the coronation of Elizabeth II.

Nick lived in Wallingford for a short time after his father died, with his mother who at the time managed The Blue Room restaurant owned by

Pettits. After their marriage, Janet and Nick remained local for a short time, initially living in Cholsey, then Appleford when Nick started work with Pressed Steel (then part of British Leyland) and finally moving to Swindon when his job moved from the headquarters at Cowley to the manufacturing plant at Swindon.

By this time Nick and Janet had decided that they and their two daughters needed a new start in life and applied for emigration to Canada which occurred in 1973. Nick is an only child and his mother remained in England while Janet's parents also emigrated after the sale of Reynolds & Johnstone. Frequent trips "back home" to England took place and although truly "Canadians" there is a part of both Nick and Janet that remains in Wallingford.

Growing up in a town like Wallingford leaves everlasting memories and many of these form the basis of stories about what "things were like" in the 1950's and 1960's - our formative years when Wallingford was home. By weaving some personal history into this book, the hope is that, although the Shepherd's have long since gone, and the Johnstone's numbers have declined, the part that the families played in the evolution of the town and the part that the town played in their own "formation" will not be completely lost for future generations.

Nick Shepherd,
Ottawa, Canada
July 2021

References and Endnotes

[1] John Kirby Hedges, 1881, The History of Wallingford in two volumes, Vol 1 to 1326, and Volume 2 1327 - 1880, Published 1881, Oxford University Press.

[2] "1155 - 1955 Wallingford Royal Charter," Souvenir brochure, quote by the original author.

[3] Base Google Maps - Wallingford High Street between Wallingford Bridge and Squash Club.

[4] Base Google Maps - Wallingford High Street focused on The Lamb crossroads.

[5] Originally posted on Facebook Group "Bygone Wallingford" and used with permission.

[6] Base map from link below and added locations of tunnels with diamonds: https://www.freecountrymaps.com/map/towns/great_britain/27532643/ attribution permission per website © copyright FreeCountryMaps.com

[7] Base map Google maps with sightings shown as diamonds

[8] Depiction of Flint House ground floor as of 1960 while being used as a warehouse for Leonard Shepherd Ltd. Partly based on "Some notes on the Domestic Architecture of Wallingford, Berkshire," P. S. Spokes, F.S.A., Berkshire Archaeological Journal Volume 50, 1947

[9] From private Shepherd family collection (later used as postcard).

[10] South Oxfordshire District Council, Wallingford Conservation Area Appraisal, https://www.southoxon.gov.uk/wp-content/uploads/sites/2/2020/11/Wallingford-Conservation-Area-Appraisal-Parts-1-3.pdf Source map under license from OS CS-222102-C3V1R4

[11] http://projectbritain.com/history.html History of Britain source for periods chosen.

[12] Wallingford Museum website at https://www.wallingfordmuseum.org.uk/

[13] https://www.romanobritain.org/1-arc/arc_roman_towns.php

[14] "Wallingford: The Castle and the Town in Context." Edited by K. S. B. Keats-Rohan, Neil Christie, David Roffe. BAR British Series 621, 2015

[15] https://www.heraldseries.co.uk/news/15186736.roman-villa-found-at-development-site-in-cholsey/ 2017 finding of Roman villa in Cholsey area.

[16] https://digventures.com/earth-trust/background/wittenham-clumps/ Background on Wittenham Clumps dig

[17] John Kirby Hedges, 1893, "A Short History of Wallingford, Ancient, Medieval, and Modern" P 134

[18] See information at https://romanlincolnshire.wordpress.com/physical-remains-lincoln/

[19] https://en.wikipedia.org/wiki/Dover_Castle some background on this location

[20] https://www.iknow-uk.com/articles/portchester-portsdown-hill notes on Portchester fort and castle as it developed.

[21] Historic UK - *The* History and Heritage Accommodation Guide with permission, www.historic-uk.com See specific page for timeline, https://www.historic-uk.com/HistoryUK/HistoryofBritain/Timeline-of-Roman-Britain/

[22] Dowding, Janka., "The Prevalence of Christianity in Roman Britain to AD 410," 2007, Hirundo (Magazine of Department of Classical Studies, McGill).

[23] https://www.hertfordshiremercury.co.uk/news/hertfordshire-news/hitchin-town-underground-tunnels-rumour-4631287 The Hertfordshire tunnels and the link with St. Mary's Church

[24] Roman Lincolnshire Revealed blog https://romanlincolnshire.wordpress.com actual page at https://romanlincolnshire.wordpress.com/physical-remains-lincoln/ History of the link to pre Norman churches in Lincoln.

[25] Used with permission. https://www.greatenglishchurches.co.uk/html/the_pre-norman_church.html provides interesting background on the evolution of churches in England.

[26] "Wallingford: The Castle and the Town in Context." Edited by K. S. B. Keats-Rohan, Neil Christie, David Roffe. BAR British Series 621, 2015, base map with added circles for key churches.

[27] Private picture taken in Church.

[28] "Thames Crossings near Wallingford from Roman to Early Norman Times," A. J. Grayson, Oxoniensia, 2010

[29] "Transforming Townscapes: From burh to borough. The archeology of Wallingford AD 800 - 1400, Neil Christie and Oliver Creighton, Kindle Books

[30] British History Online, Version 5.0. Accessed 6 May 2021. www.british-history.ac.uk. (Quote from text of Chapter 32 The College of Wallingford https://www.british-

history.ac.uk/vch/berks/vol2/pp103-106)

[31] http://www.castlesfortsbattles.co.uk/south_east/wallingford_castle.html

[32] For an account of the three sieges see "Transforming Townscapes: From burh to borough. The archeology of Wallingford AD 800 - 1400, Chapter 5.6, Neil Christie and Oliver Creighton, Kindle Books

[33] British History Online, Version 5.0. Accessed 6th May 2021. www.british-history.ac.uk. (From history of Wallingford Castle https://www.british-history.ac.uk/vch/berks/vol3/pp517-531)

[34] Castles through time tab from the English Heritage website https://www.english-heritage.org.uk/castles/castles-through-time/

[35] Janis Tubbs, "Our World For You" (extract as quoted on https://www.ourworldforyou.com/turrets-tunnels-dover-castle-england/)

[36] Story of tunnels under Dover Castle https://www.kentlive.news/news/nostalgia/secret-underground-tunnels-kent-hidden-3841354

[37] Historic England, 2021, HE research records, Historic England, viewed (07 May 2021), web address inside angular brackets <https://www.pastscape.org.uk/hob.aspx?hob_id=468096> (Heritage Gateway).

[38] http://www.sussexarch.org.uk/saaf/pevensey.html also see reference to source. (Guy 1084 P 110)

[39] Quoted from description of Figure 5.3 as shown in "Wallingford: The Castle and the Town in Context." Edited by K. S. B. Keats-Rohan, Neil Christie, David Roffe. BAR British Series 621, 2015

[40] "Wallingford: The Castle and the Town in Context." Edited by K. S. B. Keats-Rohan, Neil Christie, David Roffe. BAR British Series 621, 2015, base map with added circles for key churches.

[41] https://www.atlasobscura.com/places/nottingham-caves

[42] Headline quoted from Notts TV website story, dated August 1st 2017. https://nottstv.com/secret-tunnels-connecting-nottingham-castle-city-centre-myth/

[43] https://www.ancientpages.com/2015/12/06/secret-passageways-and-caves-beneath-the-nottingham-castle/

[44] Stories about several locations in East Anglia including many about passages under Norwich Castle. https://www.hiddenea.com/norfolkn.htm

[45] Tunnels and crypts under Norfolk Castle https://www.wingingtheworld.com/underground-norwich/

[46] Norman House and Priory references https://www.eveningnews24.co.uk/news/a-look-at-underground-norwich-1710364

[47] Source: Pamela Brooks: 'Norfolk Ghosts & Legends' (Halsgrove, 2008), P.90.

[48] https://www.bristolpost.co.uk/news/bristol-news/bristols-secret-tunnels-hidden-explore-934313

[49] Original picture, Motacilla, CC BY-SA 3.0 <https://creativecommons.org/licenses/by-sa/3.0>, via Wikimedia Commons

[50] Using Google Maps as a base showing key locations related t churches relevant to Oxford Castle.

[51] http://www.bbc.co.uk/northamptonshire/content/articles/2009/04/03/underground_northampton_tunnels_feature.shtml

[52] https://en.m.wikipedia.org/wiki/Northampton's_tunnels

[53] https://www.visitbritainshop.com/world/articles/castle-dungeons-with-an-english-heritage-pass/

[54] https://www.exploring-castles.com/castle_designs/castle_dungeon/

[55] https://www.exploring-castles.com/uk/england/pontefract_castle/

[56] http://featherstonesmad.smfforfree4.com/index.php/topic,120.0.html

[57] Pictures from Trip Advisor public site

[58] https://www.walesonline.co.uk/news/wales-news/truth-lurking-underneath-welsh-town-13618461

[59] Picture posted on Reddit approx. 2010

[60] https://www.hiddenea.com/suffolkl.htm also this site quotes sources for the story A. J. Forrest: 'Under Three Crowns' (Boydell Press, 1961), p.105. D. E. Davey: 'A Short Account of Leiston Abbey' (Baldwin, Cradock & Joy, 1823), p.9. 'The East Anglian Magazine', Vol.19, p.287. And Former weblink: www.boxvalley.co.uk/nature/sns/wad49/w49-geo.htm

[61] https://www.hiddenea.com/suffolkl.htm

[62] https://www.gazettelive.co.uk/whats-on/whats-on-news/pub-believed-home-secret-underground-12195939

[63] Reproduced courtesy of the Swindon Advertiser https://www.swindonadvertiser.co.uk/news/16978610.new-tunnels-discovered-old-town/

[64] Both maps based on Google Maps with potential speculative passageways added.

Other useful links

Wallingford History Gateway for more research studies on Wallingford
https://sites.google.com/site/wallingfordhistorygateway/Home/resources/studies

Notes on references and copyrights.

Developing this book involved both personal memories and stories from others. It also required a lot of research from historic and current publications - mostly through internet searches.

As can be seen from the length of the "end notes" many sources were used. Every effort was made to ensure that permission to use the material was granted, and in all cases where contact was made this has been granted.

If there are any situations where a reader discovers material in the book and believes that permission has not been sought, then our deep apologies, and please contact the author. In almost every case permission that was granted was at zero or minimal costs. The intent of the book has not been to make money but to document a story and hopefully to generate interest in both the potential for tunnels and passageways - but also in the special stories and history of the Town of Wallingford.

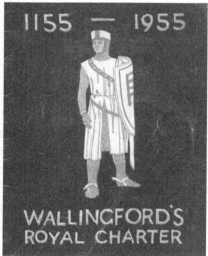